Sir John Eliot, Alexander Balloch Grosart

An apology for Socrates and Negotium posterorum : Now for the first time printed from the author's MSS. at Port Eliot

Sir John Eliot, Alexander Balloch Grosart

An apology for Socrates and Negotium posterorum : Now for the first time printed from the author's MSS. at Port Eliot

ISBN/EAN: 9783337156770

Printed in Europe, USA, Canada, Australia, Japan

Cover: Foto ©Thomas Meinert / pixelio.de

More available books at **www.hansebooks.com**

DISTRIBUTION OF THE 100 COPIES.

1. HER MAJESTY THE QUEEN.
2-11. THE RIGHT HONBLE. THE EARL ST. GERMANS, PORT ELIOT, ST. GERMANS.
12-18. THE EDITOR.
19. FREE LIBRARY, BLACKBURN, PER MR. DAVID GEDDES.
20. REV. C. W. BOASE, M.A., EXETER COLLEGE, OXFORD.
21. H. T. HAMILTON-BRUCE, ESQ., EDINBURGH.
22. HIS GRACE THE DUKE OF BUCCLEUCH, PER JAMES STEWART, ESQ.
23. ROYAL LIBRARY, BERLIN, PER MESSRS. ASHER & CO.
24. THE BODLEIAN LIBRARY, OXFORD, PER REV. H. O. COXE, M.A.
25. BALLIOL COLLEGE, OXFORD, PER REV. T. K. CHEYNE, M.A.
26. THE BRITISH MUSEUM, LONDON.
27. W. E. BRIGGS, ESQ., M.P., HARROW-ON-THE-HILL.
28. THE BOSTON ATHENÆUM, PER C. A. CUTTER, ESQ.
29. THE PUBLIC LIBRARY, BOSTON, PER MESSRS. TRÜBNER & CO.
30. THOMAS BROCKLEBANK, JUNR., ESQ., LIVERPOOL.
31. REV. SAMUEL W. BROOKS, STANMORE, SYDNEY, N. S. WALES.
32. W. CUNLIFFE-BROOKS, ESQ., MANCHESTER.
33. HENRY BRADSHAW, ESQ., M.A., UNIVERSITY LIBRARY, CAMBRIDGE.
34. THE MOST HONBLE. THE MARQUIS OF BUTE.
35. J. H. CHAMBERLAIN, ESQ., BIRMINGHAM.
36. CHETHAM LIBRARY, MANCHESTER.
37. THOMAS CHORLTON, ESQ., MANCHESTER.
38. THE RIGHT HONBLE. THE LORD CHIEF JUSTICE OF ENGLAND.

DISTRIBUTION OF COPIES.

39. BERTHA M. CORDERY, LONDON.
40. F. W. COSENS, ESQ., LONDON.
41. THE RIGHT HONBLE. VISCOUNT CRANBROOK, LONDON.
42. THE RIGHT HONBLE. THE EARL OF DERBY, KNOWSLEY.
43. HIS GRACE THE DUKE OF DEVONSHIRE, K.G.
44. THE REV. DR. DICKSON, UNIVERSITY, GLASGOW.
45. THE REV. J. W. EBSWORTH, M.A., MOLASH VICARAGE.
46. C. H. ELT, ESQ., LONDON.
47. HIS HONOUR JUDGE FALCONER, USK.
48. F. F. FOX, ESQ., CLIFTON, BRISTOL.
49. SAMUEL R. GARDINER, ESQ., M.A., LONDON.
50. H. HUCKS GIBBS, ESQ., LONDON.
51. THE RIGHT HONBLE. W. E. GLADSTONE, PRIME MINISTER.
52. HARVARD UNIVERSITY, CAMBRIDGE, BOSTON, MASS.
53. BENJAMIN HAYNES, ESQ., CLEVEDON, SOMERSET.
54. C. E. H. CHADWYCK HEALEY, ESQ., LONDON.
55. THE LORD HOUGHTON, FRYSTON HALL, FERRYBRIDGE.
56. R. HOPWOOD HUTCHINSON, ESQ., J.P., BLACKBURN.
57. DR. INGLEBY, VALENTINES, ILFORD.
58. RICHARD JOHNSON, ESQ., KEMNAL MANOR.
59. JOHN KERSHAW, ESQ., LONDON.
60. JOHN KERSHAW, ESQ., CROSS GATES, AUDENSHAW.
61. CHARLES LILBURNE, ESQ., SUNDERLAND.
62. F. DE MUSSENDEN LEATHES, ESQ., LONDON.
63. F. K. LENTHALL, ESQ., BESSALS LEIGH MANOR.
64. W. J. LINTON, ESQ., NEWHAVEN, CONN.
65. THE MOST HONBLE. THE MARQUIS OF LOTHIAN.
66. J. MANSFIELD MACKENZIE, ESQ., EDINBURGH.
67. FREE LIBRARY, OLD TOWN HALL, MANCHESTER, PER MR. C. W. SUTTON.
68. PROFESSOR MORLEY, LONDON.
69. JOHN MORISON, ESQ., GLASGOW.
70. LITERARY AND PHILOSOPHICAL INSTITUTE, NEWCASTLE-ON-TYNE, PER R. S. WATSON, ESQ.
71. HERBERT NEW, ESQ., GREENHILL, EVESHAM.
72. DR. BRINSLEY NICHOLSON, LONDON.
73. JOHN OAKEY, JUNR., ESQ., LONDON.

DISTRIBUTION OF COPIES.

74. CORNELIUS PAINE, ESQ., BRIGHTON.
75. PEABODY INSTITUTE, BALTIMORE, M'D., U.S.A., PER E. G. ALLEN, ESQ.
76. ALBERT PIKE, ESQ., WASHINGTON, U.S.A.
77. REV. JAMES PORTER, M.A., MASTER OF PETERHOUSE, CAMBRIDGE.
78. HORACE N. PYM, ESQ., LONDON.
79. THE REFORM CLUB, LONDON.
80. THE MOST HONBLE. THE MARQUIS OF RIPON.
81. MR. ROBERT ROBERTS, BOSTON, LINCOLNSHIRE.
82. REV. DR. SALISBURY, THUNDERSLEY RECTORY, SALISBURY.
83. JOHN SHELLEY, ESQ., PLYMOUTH.
84. A. G. SNELGROVE, ESQ., LONDON.
85. ALGERNON C. SWINBURNE, ESQ., LONDON.
86. THE PUBLIC LIBRARY OF VICTORIA, AUSTRALIA.
87. THE PARLIAMENT LIBRARY, VICTORIA, AUSTRALIA.
88. FREE PUBLIC LIBRARY, SYDNEY, AUSTRALIA.
89. PARLIAMENTARY LIBRARY, SYDNEY, AUSTRALIA.
90. UNIVERSITY LIBRARY, SYDNEY, AUSTRALIA.
91. C. J. THOMAS, ESQ., BRISTOL.
92. J. M. THOMSON, ESQ., EDINBURGH.
93. TRINITY COLLEGE, DUBLIN.
94. THE RIGHT HONBLE. VISCOUNT VERULAM, GORHAMBURY, ST. ALBANS.
95. R. S. WATSON, ESQ., NEWCASTLE-ON-TYNE.
96. STATE LIBRARY, WASHINGTON, PER THEODORE F. DWIGHT, ESQ.
97. JOHN WESTON, ESQ., NORTHWICH.
98. G. H. WHITE, ESQ., GLENTHORNE.
99. WILLIAM WILSON, ESQ., BERWICK-ON-TWEED.
100. B. PERKINS WRIGHT, ESQ., J.P., STAFFORD.

This is to certify that the entire impression of this work (2 vols.) has been rigidly limited to 100 copies, of which this is No..50... Proofs and waste sheets have been destroyed.

An Apology for Socrates and
Negotium Posterorum.

AN
APOLOGY FOR SOCRATES
AND
NEGOTIUM POSTERORUM:

BY SIR JOHN ELIOT.

(1590—1632.)

NOW FOR THE FIRST TIME PRINTED: FROM THE
AUTHOR'S MSS. AT PORT ELIOT.

*Edited, with Introduction and Additions from other MSS. at Port
Eliot, Notes and Illustrations, &c.*

BY THE

REV. ALEXANDER B. GROSART, LL.D., F.S.A.,

ST. GEORGE'S, BLACKBURN, LANCASHIRE.

IN TWO VOLUMES.

VOL. I.

INTRODUCTION—APOLOGY FOR SOCRATES—NEGOTIUM POSTERORUM,
PART I.—ADDITIONS AND NOTES AND ILLUSTRATIONS.

PRINTED FOR EARL ST. GERMANS AND
PRIVATE CIRCULATION ONLY.

1881.

CHISWICK PRESS:—C. WHITTINGHAM AND CO.,
TOOKS COURT, CHANCERY LANE.

CONTENTS OF VOL. I.

		PAGE
I.	List of the distribution of the 100 copies . . .	i-iii
II.	Introduction	xi-xxvi
III.	An Apology for Socrates	1-30
IV.	Negotium Posterorum, Part I.	31-126
V.	Additions from other MSS. at Port Eliot, Part I. .	127

INTRODUCTION.

AVING given in the Introduction to "The Monarchie of Man" (2 vols. 4to. 1879), a somewhat full Memoir of Sir John Eliot, I must refer thither those who wish to know the facts and circumstances of his illustrious Life; or the Reader will be abundantly rewarded who masters the inevitable source of all after-writers, viz. " Sir John Eliot : A Biography. 1590-1632. By John Forster. 2 vols. London, 1864 (Longman)." Here and now, I have to limit myself to (*a*) giving an account of the matter contained in the present volumes; (*b*) to explain the supplement of the two great MSS. herein reproduced (*for the first time*) from the other Port Eliot MSS. entrusted to me by Earl St. Germans.

(*a*) An account of the matter contained in the present volumes.

1. *An Apology for Socrates* (vol. i. pp. 1-30).

This MS. was among those that were found in his chamber in the Tower after his death. "It was the piece of writing," says FORSTER, "that seems last to have occupied him" (ii. p. 668). I doubt this. It is much more carefully and firmly written than his later MSS., and I rather think preceded at least some of these. Be this as it may, his Biographer truly observes on the occasion and purpose of it: "If his friends could have doubted his design in raising and answering such a question [*"An recte fecerit Socrates quod accusatus non responderit?"*] in these last hours, the words written within the paper removed all doubt: "Upon a Judgment in ye Court of King's Bench against ye privilege of Parl^t on a *nihil dicit*. 5°. Car." The Socrates as to whom inquiry was to be made, whether he had acted rightly in not replying to his accusers, was not an Athenian but an English philosopher. The name was a mask, which there was no attempt to disguise or conceal. The design was to ask from a later age, when the writer should be no longer accessible to praise or blame, the justice denied in his own. No immodest comparison, we may be sure, was intended by the choice of a name so illustrious. It was taken simply as that of a man who had been the subject of an unjust accusation; who, on being called to plead or defend himself, told his accusers that, so far from having offended against the laws, he had done nothing for which he did not think himself entitled to be rewarded by them; who took his sentence with uncomplaining calmness; and to whose memory a succeeding time offered late but repentant homage by decree of a statue to himself and of ignominy to his accusers" (ii. p. 669).

It needed no common measure of conviction of what

was the right thing to be and to do, for Sir John Eliot to stand out as he did, and while others were released to abide in prison. As no one could find better words wherewith to tell the proud story, I gladly draw again here upon the 'Biography', as thus: "There can be no doubt that in the early months of 1632 a great~pressure had been put upon Eliot by some of his friends to induce him to make such concession on the point of good behaviour as might render possible a compromise of his fine, and open some way to his release. At this time, all who had shared his imprisonment, whether by order of the king at the dissolution of parliament, or by sentence of the judges subsequently, were at large; under various pleas and pretences, some consideration having been extended to all. Even Walter Long, who before had been let loose to attend his wife's death-bed, and afterwards, upon his own petition, to visit his " motherless, fatherless, friendless children," was at length released. Very opportunely also, there had befallen Heath's resignation of the attorney-generalship, and the appointment to it of Noye; who, having taken as strong a part as either Selden or Eliot in the events that led to the scene of the second of March, appears to have been really anxious to promote the release of those quondam fellow agitators. But, though Selden consented to go free upon his personal guarantee to appear when called upon; though Valentine showed no indisposition at last, as Eliot expressed it, to knock at the "back door of the court"; and though the hangers-on of the court, noticing the rumour of an approaching parliament, were fain to speak of it as no unpleasant probability, "now that Noye and Selden are come on our side, and the rest of the rebels will be glad of mere conditions;" the person who comprised in himself that "rest of the rebels" still steadily refused every form of compromise involving a concession to his judges. Also believing that a parliament would come, he would suffer no point of its privilege to be in his person surrendered or betrayed" (ii. pp. 669-70).

It was under these sad and trying conditions that the 'Apology' was written. I for one do not wonder or blame that through it there is an under-tone of pain from the inability of his 'old associates' to sympathize with his 'noble obstinacy'. "It was difficult," continues Forster, "to bear such reproach, because impossible to answer it without assuming in turn the censor's office, not merely against renegades he despised, but against friends whom he esteemed; and it was this which seems to have determined him, in drawing up a final statement of his case, to divest it in outward seeming of any directness of personal allusion, by writing as if in defence of one who belonged to another country and a distant time. But the mask was not for concealment, and was worn so that any might uplift it" (ii. pp. 670-1). It must likewise be remembered that there was actual need for semi-concealment of his design, seeing that at any moment the king on some sudden whim of vengefulness might sweep the Prisoner's room of all his papers and with monkey-like maliciousness and mischievousness seek occasion against him as pseudo-warrant for still more inexorable treatment.

In the 'Biography' successive quotations are made from the 'Apology'—not, I am bound to say, always accurately or so carefully as they might have been—but as the complete Manuscript is now furnished *in extenso*, and in absolute integrity, it seems inexpedient to give these in this Introduction, even for the advantage of the connecting words and notes. But I cannot withhold the close: "The close is very affecting. Speaking of the sufferings, "the passions" of Socrates, he checks himself. To him only were known all the secrets of the prison in which the Socrates of whom he wrote was immured. At the time he was writing, an order from the Council had finally debarred future access from his friends; and the end, though perhaps he knew it not, was very near. But less of himself than of his countrymen he was thinking then. "Should I enumerate his passions, I should renew your griefs. I should wound you, O Athenians; I should pierce the soul of your affections with his memory." He would not, therefore, tell them what their Socrates had suffered. What he suffered in his fortune, what he suffered in his person, in his liberty, in his life, he would not relate. "To be made poor and naked; to be imprisoned and restrained; nay, not to be at all, not to have the proper use of anything; not to have knowledge of society; not to have being and existence; his faculties confiscate, his friends debarred his presence; himself deprived the world; I will not tell you all this suffered by your Socrates, and all suffered in your service; for you, most excellent Athenians, for your children, your posterity; to preserve your rights and liberties, that, as they were the inheritance of your fathers, from you they might descend to your sons." But though he sought not to move their sorrow for him of whom he wrote, he craved their justice. Of defections from the law, of contempt for authority and justice, of desertion of his own innocence, of a betrayal of the public liberties, Socrates had been accused. Was he guilty? Or had he proved his right to have preferred to die, with refusal to admit the jurisdiction of his judges, rather than to live, with such concession to an unlawful power as might have challenged and obtained their pity? The appeal was heard, and the answer given, far sooner than Eliot might have looked for in the gloom that surrounded him; at the time apparently more hopeless from some gleams of hope which had preceded it" (ii. pp. 682-3).*

I feel a not unbecoming pride that at long-last this historically priceless and biographically infinitely pathetic 'Apology' is for ever rescued from the hazards of a solitary Manuscript. Had it come down to us in Greek out of the prison-house of an Aristides—imprisoned, not banished—it had been placed beside the 'Phædo'. As it is, if it be without the dulcet words and finely-wrought phrasing of "the speech of the gods," it has a tranquil dignity, a fine restraint, an exquisite truthfulness, ay, and a natural brokenness of utterance that in my judgment ought hence-

---

* Throughout I give Forster's quotations in his text. Comparison with mine will show even in his most careful places how he tampers with words and forms.

forward to stamp it as one of the great possessions of our History and Literature. That it should have been possible for such a man as Charles I. so to deal with such a man as Sir John Eliot, is of the mysteries of Providence, and is a measure for us to-day of the broad-based liberties of 'this England'—liberties that our ELIOTS and HAMPDENS and PYMS and CROMWELLS magnanimously asserted and the Nation won. They are recreant Englishmen who side with the king—and such a king!—against the kingdom. They are the victims of a superstition, who hold for monarchy in a Charles I. as if in an Alfred, in a Charles II. as if in an Elizabeth, in George IV. as if in William III. Our present titular 'monarchy', with such a Queen as Victoria (God bless her!), is the freest and noblest existing sovereignty; but supreme over all is "The Monarchy of Man"; and no unworthy king, no fresh Charles I., or II., or George IV. would be tolerated. Nor would the revolution—*in such case*—cost what prior have done. But may a long line of descent from Victoria and Albert, 'worthily' fill our England's mighty throne!

2. *Negotium Posterorum* (vol. i. pp. 31-126: vol. ii. pp. 1-109).

As JOHN FORSTER was the first literary Worker who had unreserved access to the Port Eliot MSS., so he had the distinguished honour of being the first to sort and sift the confused mass—long neglected—of the family Papers. Under his personal direction the whole were classified and bound fittingly in noble tomes. They form such an array of historical documents and memorials as might make any Library famous. Long may they find an honoured place in the great patriot-statesman's mansion!

While justly proud of all his researches among these MSS., the Biographer to the last used to discourse, garrulously yet pleasantly, of his pre-eminent recovery (if discovery were not his preferred word) of the ' Negotium Posterorum.' One can excuse his ' magnifying' of his part in the supreme ' find.' Hitherto he had worked very much in the dark; and lo! a shaft of light flashed over the entire field.

I very willingly let him tell his own story of this inestimable Manuscript—now, like the 'Apology for Socrates,' for the first time printed *in extenso*:—" A period of Eliot's life [1625] has now arrived where guidance is happily vouchsafed to us, which we may accept without a misgiving. Among the papers at Port Eliot in his own handwriting, and of which the authorship is as manifestly his, exists a memoir of the first parliament of Charles the First.

" That this manuscript, possessing great historical importance and an unrivalled personal interest, should have failed to attract any kind of notice for more than two centuries, which have yet been filled with a vivid interest for the subject it relates to, and with enquirers eager for any scrap of authentic information concerning it, is one of those accidents that not unfrequently attend old family papers.

" Its appearance is not inviting; it is on the face of it a fragment, or intended portion of a larger work ; and it bears a Latin title, of which the meaning is not immediately perceived. But upon examination it is found to be in itself complete; to contain a narrative of every incident and debate in the Lower House, during its two sittings at Westminster and Oxford; and to include besides admirable summaries of the leading speeches, reports of every speech delivered [in the Parliament at Westminster and Oxford of Charles I., 1°] by Eliot himself.

"The object with which it was composed declares itself beyond any question. It was designed, evidently, to stand as a portion of a work that should relate to other generations the parliamentary labours and struggles in which Eliot and his friends of that existing generation had been engaged.

"Its plan would doubtless have embraced the parliaments of James in which he sat, as well as those in which he took part under Charles; and the unfinished state in which the manuscript of the "second" portion, as it is termed, reaches us, might have suggested its date, even if internal proofs did not determine it positively. At the close of the first stormy session of the great parliament of 1628, during the recess when Buckingham was murdered and Wentworth went over to the Court, it appears to have been begun; though not likely to have been brought into the state in which we find it, until the author's later imprisonment. It probably then assumed the double character—of a memorial of the struggles by which the ancient liberty had been reasserted, and of a monument to sufferings undergone in so wresting the petition of right from the king. The fulfilment of the design was interrupted by death;

and how far it had proceeded, even, cannot with certainty be said. It is quite probable that this second part comprises all that was ever written, as undoubtedly it is all now remaining at Port Eliot; though the fact of many books and manuscripts having been lost or destroyed when the mansion was repaired forty years ago leaves it doubtful whether some of the Patriot's papers may not also then have perished. More cannot be known; but in what has survived we have the record, not insufficient, however incomplete, of the opening scenes of one of the greatest conflicts in which the men of one generation ever engaged to secure the happiness and freedom of generations that were to follow. In the very title given to his manuscript by Eliot, that idea appears. Not for ourselves we did these things, made these sacrifices, underwent these toils and sufferings; but for you. It was not our own business we were then transacting, but yours—*Negotium Posterorum*" (vol. i. pp. 209-11).

At this point I intercalate two observations:

(*a*) An examination of *Negotium Posterorum* as now reproduced with all fidelity to the original MS., brings these points before us—viz. that in vol. i. page 39 (following the introductory paper, pp. 33-38) are these words—

Negotium Posterorum
Tomus Secundus, Liber Primus.

And again in vol ii. page 1, is this:—

Negotium Posterorum
Tomus Secundus, Liber Secundus.

Studying these, it seems morally certain that a 'Tomus

Primus' had been written by the author. No one would now dream of either entitling a volume 'Tomus Secundus' with a 'Tomus Primus' non-existent, or of writing 'Tomus Secundus' before 'Tomus Primus.' I therefore fear that it is beyond all doubt that a 'Tomus Primus' has perished, and perished irrevocably.

But (*b*) other MSS. of Sir John Eliot at Port Eliot contain at least portions of *materials* for such a 'Tomus Primus.' They also contain the authorities utilized in 'Tomus Secundus.' With respect to the latter, whilst we cannot make up for the prodigious loss of 'Tomus Primus,' we are able to elucidate and illustrate the events and circumstances of (strictly) a Jacobean parliament, and also to give first-hand copies of Speeches delivered by Sir John Eliot; some with greater detail than in *Negotium Posterorum*, some that were prepared but not delivered, and other relative documents. Of these, in the sequel.

The Biographer quotes largely from *Negotium Posterorum*. If I cannot accept absolutely his assurance that "the Reader may rely with perfect confidence on the scrupulous precision and accuracy with which all that is essential in this remarkable manuscript . . . is laid before him," it is because I deem integrity of wording to be the 'essential of essentials.' Nevertheless, regarded broadly, Forster has made effective use of this MS. for *his* purpose. I cannot but rejoice, however, that the historical student has the great MS. now before him, as the author intended it to reach him; *id est*, not cut up into fragments and snippets taken hither and thither, but in completeness.

To myself *Negotium Posterorum* has the solemnity of a Greek play. Beginning with the sunny welcome to Charles on the death of his mean and meagre, though shrewd and (in a sense) learned father (James I.), and the generous hopes of the foremost in the nation in and for him, all too swiftly ominous shadows fall in black bands and bars across the sunshine and the gladness. The Turks (*mirabile dictu!*) were harassing the coasts and even harbours of England; and there was terrible internal misery and discontent. The stage is early seen to be too vast for the poor Players on it. Buckingham is the Fate of the young king—perchance his heaviest paternal heritage. Following on the great sigh of relief to all England over the shattering of the 'Spanish Marriage' scheme, came his ill-advised election of 'Maria,' which all the glamour of courtly poets never succeeded (or could succeed) in transmuting into English 'Mary.' Then behind, above, encompassing all, there is revealed an innate ineradicable shiftiness and treachery to his spoken and written word, on the part of the king, a constant playing fast and loose with truth, a perpetual 'promising to the ear' and falsification in the act. And so the 'Debates' in the House are coloured by the atmosphere and lights and shadows in which they are held. Anything more despicable, more un-English than Charles's dealing in the matter of Bishop Montagu—to name a lesser thing first—or in the central difficulty of 'Subsidies'—to accentuate a greater thing—is inconceivable. There is a certain pathos of fatality in his unvarying doing of the wrong thing and at the wrong time even for the success of it. One is awed, indeed, before the spectacle of a man so (mis)guided by a conscience perverted in its very core, whereby the poor and shallow thing of shallowest natures, obstinacy, was mistaken for august WILL. Than the account of the interview between Sir John Eliot and Buckingham (vol. i. pp. 111-112) I know nothing holding in it elements for highest imaginative-poetic treatment, if only the man were forthcoming. The unhappy Duke's 'No' to the patriot's pleading, marks a turning-point in English history. There are other dramatic possibilities—as of Sir John Eliot on the spur of the moment facing 'the Favorite' and by sheer force of his own indignation compelling him to withdraw; and the like 'answering' of the renegade Wentworth, as he truckled and cajoled, bartering his magnificent dower of intellect and many-sided power for poorest 'mess of pottage.' The long patient insistence of 'the Commons,' the firm holding to 'law and right,' the absolute determination to be true to the Nation's interests, and the fine courtesy and reluctant severity with which 'grievances' are presented, thrill one to-day, unless lukewarm water and not living blood be in the veins. The Speeches of the Leaders found in *Negotium Posterorum* take their place in the successive crises of danger and forbearing opportunity, like so many Choruses of old. I feel assured that not a few of these—as those of the fiery and brave-spoken Sir Robert Philips—will come as a revelation to many. Then —as already noted—Wentworth and the other 'opposites' to the patriots, earlier and later burst upon us in

Negotium Posterorum with all the vividness and power of actual life. Taken as a whole, however looked at, *Negotium Posterorum* is a *unique* historical-biographical work. From beginning to end, and with every abatement because of its not unfrequently cumbrous and unskilful workmanship in phrasing, we read breathlessly and with the zest of a vital Novel of Scott, or Charlotte Brontë, or George Eliot.

As a Supplement to the 'Apology for Socrates,' and 'Negotium Posterorum' I have added an Appendix to each of these volumes, of important MSS. from the Port Eliot Papers, nearly all hitherto unprinted, though quoted from and referred to by Forster. The Reader will find it special recompense to study these.

The Supplement Additions speak for themselves, but there is one document now first fully printed, on which a remark seems called for, viz., the great Speech given in vol. i. (pp. 140-148). I have inadvertently stated (p. 140) that this Speech does not appear in *Negotium Posterorum*. It really does so, though in such an imperfect and broken form as to be scarcely recognizable. If the Reader will turn to our vol. ii. pp. 85-91, and compare the text with that in our Supplement (i. 140-48) he will be grateful for the latter. Sir John Eliot must himself (and others as well) have attached unusual importance to this Speech, inasmuch as not only have we the two transcripts as printed by me, but another in Lansdowne MSS. (491, fol. 155) and the printed version in *Cottoni Poſthuma*, which is blunderingly assigned to Sir Robert Cotton. Singularly enough, Mr. Forster quotes from these latter the introductory sentences as *not* being among the Eliot MSS. This is a mistake, as our text shows (vol. i. pp. 140-1); they are in their place in the transcript, carefully and critically revised by Sir John Eliot. Mr. Samuel Rawson Gardiner, in his " Buckingham and Charles I " (i. 289), argues that this Speech was undelivered. But in *Negotium Posterorum*, Sir John expressly tells us not only that the Speech was delivered, but the effect it produced, as thus —" this inflam'd the affection of the house, & pitcht it whollie on the imitation of their ffathers " (vol. i. p. 91). This is to me decisive. But it is (barely) possible that all the " precedents " and details of the fuller Speech, were not spoken. Intrinsically, the interest and weight of the Speech is unaffected by delivery or non-delivery.

Having named the Historian Mr. Gardiner, I take the opportunity to refer every Student of the period to his most matterful and judicial volumes, commencing with his " History of England from the Accession of James I. to the Disgrace of Chief-Justice Coke, 1603-1616 " (2 vols. 8vo. 1863), and still happily being continued. On all the events and names embraced in the present volumes, Mr. Gardiner will never be consulted in vain.

It would have needlessly extended my own Notes and Illustrations to have annotated the many historical facts and names that are recorded in *Negotium Posterorum*. I have identified most; and for more Mr. Gardiner and Mr. Forster must be read. I owe Mr. Gardiner hearty thanks for his kindness in answering my (I fear) troublesomely numerous questions.

d

I will only add that as in all my books I have striven to be faithful in my reproduction of these difficult MSS. I feel it to be an honour to have been entrusted by Lord St. Germans with the task of love of giving to historical students these MSS. and those that are to succeed (in other two similar volumes), viz. *De Jure Majestatis*, with (probably) other additions of a valuable kind from his UNPUBLISHED CORRESPONDENCE, &c. &c. These additional volumes are now in the press, and may be expected some time this year. Henceforward, there will be no excuse for ignorance of the life-story and life-work of the foremost of the Worthies of our England.

ALEXANDER B. GROSART.

ST. GEORGE'S VESTRY,
BLACKBURN, LANCASHIRE.

I.
APOLOGIE FOR SOCRATES,
BEING A
VINDICATION
OF
SIR JOHN ELIOT
BY
HIMSELF.

NOTE.

See our Introduction for an account of the MS. volume preserved at Port Eliot from which this remarkable 'Apologie' is derived.—G.

APOLOGIE FOR SOCRATES.

An recte fecerit Socrates, quod accufatus non refponderit.
[*Orat. fuit. ad imitationem Max. Tirr. differt.* xxxix.]

STAND now heer (moft excellent Athenians) as a rare Character, & example, both of y^r pietie, & Juftice: of y^r Juftice, in thefe tymes, that truth may have admifsion to the publicke ear, & veiw, to the tribunall of y^r iudgments: of y^r pietie, that an Apologie maie be heard for SOCRATES, now dead, why liveinge he neglected it; that y^u will yett receave for his memorie a defence, why he defended not his innocence, & grant that vnmatcht integritie of his, his integritie & fidelitie to y^{u}wards, a vindicacon from their enemies, an expiation from their flaunders, those fcandalous afpersions whereby Socrates, & his dutie have been ftaind: & this to be done by me, the weakeft of all others, yett soe farr acceptable, as it is done for him: & that in this manner, in this sacred afsemblie, the people soe seldome celebrat,/ & convented. it is a rare

example of y^r pietie; & as to me an hono^r in the fruition of this p^rfense; soe even to Socrates though dead, a happinefse, & favour; & an admiracon vnto all men. I know not whether y^r obligacon in a iuft counterpoife & weight, wilbe greater vpon Socrates, or me: on Socrates, that his memorie is yett soe pretious in y^r eyes, that through all thefe mifts, and clouds wch have obfcur'd it, y^u have ftill a veiw, & profpect on that obiect: on me; that I fhould be thought worthie to fpeake before y^r excellencies, to fpeake in the caufe of Socrates. pardon me Socrates this high, & great prefumption, to vndertake this worke, wch is only ffitt for Hercules; to put my fhoulder to that burden, that sacred burden, of thy vertues, wch none but Atlas cann fupport; nothinge but his wifdome, *qui et cælestium & subterranearum rerum habet cognitionem,* as the antients/ faind that Giant. pardon me Socrates this tranfcendent bouldnefse, to tender my indeavours to that labour. pardon me y^u Athenians, that thus farr I intrude, (though by yr leaves) vpon y^r eares, & patience. all my hope is that, in the caufe of Socrates his Genius will afsist me, that to defend the innocence of Socrates, Socrates Eloquence will attend me: that in the Apologie of his action, I shall have the secrett influence of his iudgment; & that I know would give y^u fatiffaccon; of wch some hope I have, & wthout wch I should vtterlie difpaire. yett this I muft petition from y^r candor, that yr expectacon be the leaft: that my weakenefse may be the obiect of that facultie; not that wonder of abilitie in Socrates: that soe Socrates may be wthout p^riudice in his vertues, if the ftreames be not anfwearable to that fountaine: & if ther flow what may relifh of that spring, what that pure spirit of Socrates/ may suggeft, that it may seem the more Page 4. pretious in y^r iudgments, the more acceptable being vnlook't for.

I know the great difficultie of this worke, this apologie for Socrates, & the ftrong oppofition it will have; that in this, *That Socrates did not anfwear the accufacon made ag^t him*, ther are many enemies fuppof'd. firft *a defection from the Law, in declinninge of hir procefse*. next, *a contempt of iuftice*, in not fubmitting to authoritie, wher a rule & iudgment did command it. then *a defertion of his innocence*, in expofing that to fcandall, wch yett noe good man will fupport. & laft, *a betrayinge of y^r liberties*, that ineftimable iewell of y^r rights, involv'd in the caufe of Socrates: that Socrates by his filence, became a traitor to his country, a traitor vnto y^u, a traitor to himfelfe. all thefe crimes are charg'd vpon this one act of Socrates, or rather this neglect, *that Socrates did not anfwear*, wherein the detraction of his enemyes, ye malice/ of his accufers, Page 5. the cuninge of the informers, the corruption of the iudges; *melitus litem qui intendit, Anytus qui detulit, Lyco qui propofuit*, & the reft, doe all concurr in this, to deprave this worke of Socrates, to heighten it to thefe crimes; to make him guiltie of offence, whofe offence was only, not to have [been] guiltie; & by the condemnacon of his virtue to raife a iuftificacon for their vice.

to encounter all thefe powers, I know, is a worke of difficultie: to anfweare all thefe crimes, to give satisfaccon in thefe charges; for their number, for their weight, requires noe little labour: to vindicate the honor & reputation of Socrates, in this danger, & necefsitie it is in, is a tafke even fitt for Socrates; his Eloquence, & wifedome were he liveinge, & his fpirit only, & genius, now he's dead. one word of Socrates would fuffice it; one found, & articulation of his voice; thofe few fillables, *his Innocence*, haveinge the grace/ of that exprefsion wch his tongue would give them, that mellifluous tongue of his; that one word, pafsing through his lips, would anfwear all obiections, his defence were full in that: though the eares of all men were sealed vp, & an obftruccon in their heareing, yett the aer would regulate the motion of that sound to the figures ot his truth; it would be ther read written in the aer, & (though mens affections did refufe it) the aer would ther retaine it; to the veiw, and wounder of pofteritie. But Socrates being dead, that word has loft his vertue, to wch the realitie gives power. the innocence of Socrates, haveing influence on the word, would have made it soe prevalent, & effective: but now that p'fection beinge wantinge, ther being noe paralell of that virtue, the fillables want ther harmonie, they ftrike not that affection in the hearers, by the concord & diapafion of their speeche, and therefore/ larger arguments muft be vf'd, by p'ticulars to prove it: by p'ticular anfweares, to the p'ticular obiections that are made; by p'ticular defences, to each p'ticular charge; & soe from a speciall apologie in dark crime to implie his iuftificacon in the generall. This method I shall follow wherein I muft crave y^r favours to accompanie me,

APOLOGIE FOR SOCRATES.

y^r attenſions to obſerve ye tract & levell of my reaſon : y^r patience to afford me tyme, & libertie, in this ſubiect; y^r wiſedomes (moſt excellent Athenians) to ſupplie the defect of my expreſsion, wher my mouth shall prove (as in this caſe I fear it much) to[o] naʀrow for my hart, & yr pardon for thoſe errors I committ, wch my weakneſse, my ignorance, want of memory, & confidence, will in part extenuat & excuſe: the glorie of this p^{r}ſence,/ this rare concourſe, and aſsemblie of the people, beinge an obiect soe excellent, that wth a raviſhing delight it captivats my ſence; & in stead of intention on my worke takes me wholie in wonder & admiration. but to p'pare & facilitat the waie in this great iorney and adventure to wch y^r favors doe encourage me; I muſt praie y^u to looke backe, to reflect a litle, on the courſe, & proceedings firſt wth Socrates : Page 8.

the firſt ſtate, & meritt of his cauſe, wch will give an illustra-con to the reſt. ſomethinge may thence ariſe for the matter of apologie, wch I know yr pietie will not barr me; or if to me, yett y^u will not to Socrates denie it. his virtue ſhall not be p^{r}cluded of y^t help, wch is the common rule of Juſtice in all caſes, to give a free scope, & libertie of argument, to admitt all cercumſtance of vſe; much more then maie I p^{r}ſume it, at y^r handes, whoe are moſt iuſt, yea like iuſtice in the abſtract; & in this caſe for Socrates;/ whoſe example y^u held soe pretious whileſt he lived, & now his memory, being dead. Socrates was accuſ'd to have spoken divers things in Senat, divers things by waie of greivance, & complaint : some things againſt Melitus, who after was his iudge; some things ag^t Anytus, who had the p'ſecution of his cauſe; Page 9.

some things againſt Lyco, the informer, from whom the delation did p'ceed, & others of y^t leven; but all ſhrowding under ye canopie of the State, all caſting themſelves wthin the proteccon of y^t buckler, and ther fightinge wth our Hector, as Troilus under Aiax; what for diſquſicon he p'pounded againſt them, turninge it to ſedicon in the goverment; intitleing ye goverment to all their enormities and exorbitance, & tranſlating the complaints/ againſt themſelves, to y^e ſlaunder of the goverment. for this Socrates was accuſed, & thus his charge was laid, thus to have spoken againſt y^u, but wth refleccon on the ſtate; wth intencon to have wounded the head in thoſe ill members; through their ſides to have made a penetracon to the hart, & this in publicke senate, in that sacred ſanctuary of your liberties, wher iuſtice is soe religiouſlie profeſt, that noe faulte scapes unpuniſhed. In this Socr[ates] displead the priviledge of ye Senat. that noe leſser court had iuriſdicon in that cauſe, that from all antiquitie ther had been a conſtant poſseſsion of that right, wthout any violacon or impeach^t. divers reaſons, & authorities he product, for the cleering of y^t intereſt./ that though all things had been true, as they were given in the suggeſtion, and Socrates had been faultie (wch noe man can fuſpect) though to the outward ſubſtance of his actions that inward forme, & ſiniſter intention had been added; yett he was no wher puniſhable, noe wher queſtionable but in that Court, by that iudgm^t of the Senate, the ſentence of y^t place, wher noe delinquent could inioye impunitie, ſoe long to be elſwhere obnoxious to a queſtion. for confirmacon of y^t priviledge fower ſorts of authorities were vs'd, all pregnaunt in the pointe, all bindeinge vpon Socrates. firſt ye claimes and challenges of Senat, layinge it as a ground & poſition of their birthright. next the reſolucons of the iudges, the ordinary/ iudges of the law, ſuch as Melitus & the like, cohſentinge, & approving of that right. then the allowance, and conceſsion of all princes who ſtill doe acknowledge and confirme it. then Lawes and ſtatutes in the pointe, tyinge both Socrates and others, to the ſtrickt obſervance of y^t intereſt. and laſtly a p^rſident, and example, to demonſtrat it. to wch add, the reaſons, for Socrates his ſaftie, and integritie, that however, *in foro ivdicij*, he were free, yett *in foro conſcientiæ*, he was bound ; that the great iudgm^t of Socrates did oblidge him to inſiſt vpon this priviledge, to p^rſerve this publicke right ; tellinge him ſtill in private, in the Cabanet of his hart, that it was the due of Senators, & by ſubmiſsion to the contrary/ he ſhould be conſcious of their p'iudice; he ſhould be guiltie of the violation of that priviledge ; of the violacon of his duty, though others had otherwiſe determined it : & that in future he ſhould ſtand obnoxious to the Senate for that act of p^riudice and violacon ; & ſoe by declinninge the danger of that tyme which might have reparacon in another, incurr the cenſure of another wch could have reparacon in noe tyme. But to make this more p'ſpicuous, cleerly to ſtate ye caſe, I ſhall crave leave to inſtance ſome p'ticulars : for by the groundes & inducements then in Socrates, we ſhall beſt iudg the ſcope of his intentions. by the intention cheifely ſhall we come to the true knowledge of his acts, wch may be worth^y of praiſe, or condemnacon, accordinge to the

Page 12.

Page 13.

10   *APOLOGIE FOR SOCRATES.*

Page 14.

pet. prol. in primo Senat.

Page 15.

11 R. 2. rot. par n⁰. 7.

ſpirit/ that did guide them. ffor the claimes and challenges of the Senate they are numberleſſe, & manie; and the conceſsions as frequent by the princes, repeated in all ages, at the initiation of all meetings; wher the peticon is ſtill made (not of grace, but right) for yᵗ immunitie in p'ticular, *that if in that Senat any did offend they ſhould be only puniſhed in that place, that noe arreſt ſhould be, or impeachment of their p'ſons, for matters and agitacons in that ſphear;* (much leſſe a iudgmᵗ & queſtion for their lives) wᶜʰ as the proper right of Senators, the common right of Athens, the antient birthright, & inheritance of yʳ fathers, thoſe famous fathers, and founders, of yʳ greatneſse (moſt prudent, and moſt excellent Athenians) has been ſtill granted, and allowed; ſoe as that number or order may afford, what tyme & approbacon/ maie creat, in the opinion of this priviledge, Socrates had it heer, in theſe claimes, and recognitions, to wᶜʰ almoſt all places, & all perſons might atteſt. but if vſe & cuſtome, wᶜʰ is in other things equevalent to law, & creats a right; be not in this caſe ſufficient to confirme it: if the familiaritie in that, like the common vſe of oders, have dull'd the apprehenſion of our ſenſe, we haue varietie p'fented in the allegations wᶜʰ he made, out of the antient Rhetra of yr lawes, wherein it is expreſt vpon the occaſion of thoſe tymes, *that all great matters mov'd in ſenate ought to be handled diſcuſsed and adiudged onlie by courſe of senate and not in inferiour Courts,* to wᶜʰ right & declaracon the prince conſented and approved. as likewife afterwardes vpon an appeale of treaſon in that Court; the lawiers, & men ſkillfull in thoſe ſtuddies, being conſulted did confefse, that, moveinge in that place, it was not w^{th}in their notion, w^{h}in the compafse of their/ cognifance; & there- vpon concluded *that by the antient cuſtome it appertayned, to the franchiſe & liberties of the ſenate to iudge of what was moveinge in that orbe, & that noe other Courts had iuryſdiccon in ſuch caſes, wch Courts did only execute the ordinances & eſtabliſhments of senate, and not iudg the senate, or priviledges thereof.* to the like he urged a proteſtacon of that Counſell vpon an occaſion of ſome fear, *that it was the antient and vndoubted birthright and inheritance of ye Athenians freelie to treat, reaſon & debate all matters, & buſineſses in Senate, w'out any impeachment, impriſonment, or moleſtacon, other then the censure of that Court,* wch ſhews the right, claime, and pofseſsion of the Senate, and that firſt ground, and foundacon on wch Socrates did build. the next was, the reſoluc̃ons of ye iudges, the iudges of ould tyme, whoſe wiſedomes, & integrities p^rferr'd them, wher they were concurringe in this pointe (and neuer/ any differd from that sence, but such as were spoken by their ends, to be vnworthy of thoſe names, whoſe retractions were after written in their bloodes) the reſoluc̃ons of thoſe elders, thoſe worthyly calld iudges, are the next authoritie he brings; whereof two are moſt remarkable; the firſt on a queſtion of precedence, only a title of prioritie in that place, whereon all thoſe sages being conſulted, all the iudges calld to deliver their opinions, they anſweared; *that, it being matter of the Senate, belong'd wholy to y^t priviledge, and ought to be ther decided, & not elſwher.* & if not a privat queſtion of p^rcedence how much leſse the publicke buſineſse

Page 16.

rot. process. &
Judic. 11 R. 2.

18 Ja[mes].

Page 17.

11. R. 2.

27. H. 6.
rot. par no.
18.

of that howfe? the second was vppon ye imprifonment of a member, a member of that body, wher the iudges likewife being confulted, (*after fad communicacon, & mature deliberacon had*, as 'twas voucht from the words of the authoritie) anfweared *that it belonged not to them to determine of thofe high/ priviledges;* for wch they affignd two reafons drawne from ye power & cuftome of that Counfell, *that it had not been vf'd afore tyme*, and *that the Senate was a Court foe high, & mightie in its nature, that it could make law, and, that wch was law, it could make to be none*. where both in the affirmative, & negative, it is cleer, for the inducement of our Socrates, that what concernes either the priviledge, or bufineffe of ye Senate (and in the bufinefse the greateft priviledge is imported) muft haue decifion in that place, & in no other; in none that is inferior. his next ground, and reafon, was drawne from the lawes and ftatutes of this Country, thofe ould rules by wch Athens has been happie in a long continuance of profperitie (& long may it foe continue euen to the envie of hir enemyes, the admiracon of hir frendes) thofe lawes, thofe inftruments of felicitie/ are the next ground of that silence in our Socrates, wherein he finds not only reafon to excufe him, but authoritie commanding him, not to attempt the contrary, vpon the perill of his iudgment. & what might follow the violacon of his duty. and what greater danger vnto Socrates, then the hafard of his faith, that publicke faith, and fidelitie he ought to his Country, to the Senate, to the lawes, to y^r moft sacred lawes, and liberties ô Athenians? what greater danger vnto Socrates then a violacon of this duty? what greater obligation then his confcience? both wch were necefsitated in this one act of Socrates, that to fecure himfelfe in either, his silence was enforct, both for the obligacon, and the danger. The lawes wch he infifted on were two (& thefe likewife y^u may see recorded in y^r Rhetra) the firft concludinge in termes pofitive, & definit, *that noe member of the Senate/ ought to be queftion'd for any bill, speakinge, reafoninge, or declaring in that place,* wch is a cleer illuftracon of the right, a cleer demonftration of the priviledg, that, what ther was in agitation, was not queftionable elfwher; and therefore Socrates in his duty to that priviledge, in obfervance of that right, could not before his Judges, make anfweare to the fact, wch he was charg'd foe to haue done in Senate, leaft he admitt their iurifdiccon, contrary to that law. the second is more bindeinge, and seemes to have been p'pared as a proper remedie for this sore, this wound wch Socrates did suftaine: & therein the p'vifion is not only, for the securitie of Socrates from abroad, that he be not elfewher queftioned for matters done in Senate; but likewife, from w^thin, that noe informacon lie againft him, noe intelligence doe pafse, vppon the secretts of his iudgmentes, & what overtures/ he makes in the afsembly of that Councell for the publicke service, and advantage: that ther be noe difcovery made vpon him. and this, as it bindes vp others, not to difcover Socrates; foe it ingages Socrates, both for himfelfe, & others, not to difcouer them. for it recites, that *wher some to advance themfelves had given intelligence of certaine matters mov'd in Senat, before they were ther accorded, & foe*

Page 20.
4 H. 8.

Page 21.

2 H. 4 rot.
par no. 11.

cauf'd a p'ticular diflike againft their fellowes, & a generall p'iudice to the publicke p'ceedings of that Counfell. therefore it enacts to p'vent that evill in future, *that none fhuld soe inform, & that noe faith or creditt should be given them if they did.* wherein (as the iuftice of Melitus is apparant that receav'd the informacon againft Socrates, and the integritie of Lyco y^t informed/ him, and the office of Anytus that accufed him) the dutie likewife of Socrates is expreft, that he might not make difcovery of thofe pafsages, that he might not open what had been in agitacon in the Senat, and therefore could not anfwear, when his anfwear muft implie the intelligenc of thofe fecretts. ther was yett farther, another ground of Socrates, befides thefe lawes, refolucõns, claimes, and concefsions of all tymes (wherein the right is evident) wch alfo proves the vfe, the pofsefsion of that right; & that is a iudgment in the pointe, where ye contrary had been actuat, wher an attempt was made in p'iudice of this priviledge, the support of ye liberties [of] the Senate. The cafe was this, a private p'fon of this Cittie, for exhibiting a bill in Senat wch pointed at the limit, & reformacon of some great ones, had afterwardes/ by the Judges a fentence *læfæ maieftatis* given againft him, but the Senat, in their next meetinge, findeinge this sentence grounded vpon what had its motion in that fphear, and that the partie had been queftion'd wthout them ; they thervpon, (wthout entring into the meritts of the caufe, wthout confideracon of the fact whither it had such guilt, but fimplie) for their priviledg *pro*

intereſſe suo, as the Rhetra has it, for the pᵣſervacon of their
liberties, to maintaine that antient right, *that in such caſes
none were queſtionable but by them, & in yᵉ this vs done
wᵗʰout them, that it was made the iuriſdiccon of another,*
vpon this error that sentence was reverſd, & a iudgment
made to fruſtrat and annihil it, in confirmacon of the
priviledg of Senate, and this in a caſe of treaſon, & for one
that was not a member/ of that Counſell, how much more
then is that immunitie extendinge, that priviledg belonginge
vnto Socrates, and in a caſe more qualified, wherein leſse
danger is pᵣtended? Socrates on this conceaved himſelf
diſcharg'd in pointe of right, & equitie; naie he conceav'd
that right, to haue a ſtrickt obligacon on his conſcience, yᵗ
from him ther ſhould come nothinge wᶜʰ might pᵣiudice
it : & this was an interdiccon to his anſwear, a ſuper-
ſedeas to that aſt, and therefore Socrates made his Cataſ-
trophe in ſilence, & wᵗʰ theſe reaſons that silence was
induſt. in wᶜʰ whither Socrates were guiltie; guiltie of
thoſe crimes wᶜʰ are obiected to him; guiltie of any;
guiltie of all; whether that whole ſtreame of malidicon
fall worthily on his memorie, now that Socrates is dead,/
or any drop might iuſtlie light vpon him; or the innocence,
& integritie of our Socrates, on the Contrerry, should yett
be free from all, is now the queſtion of this daie, the
obieſt of yʳ intentions, the ſubieſt of my endeavʳˢ wherein
(moſt excellent Athenians) as you will grant yʳ attentions
vnto me, I muſt againe peticon yʳ retentions for dead
Socr[ates] : that yʳ love, and affeſtion to his virtues, may
cover the imperfeſtions of his servant : he that now labours

1 H. 4. rot.
pᵃʳ no. 104.

Page 24.

Page 25.

againſt ſoe many difficulties, both of perſons, and the tyme, & the deceipts, & fallacies of either, yett to render truly y^r Socrates to y^u, y^u vnto y^r Socrates. to this end, I ſhall now applie my ſelfe, to the p'ticulars charg'd againſt him, wth his defence in each p'ticular; each p'ticular crime ſhall have p'ticular anſwears, & all I hope their ſatiſſaccon in

Page 26. the generall, that none/ ſhall be left doubtfull vpon Socrates, noe ſpot vnwaſht that may be an aſperſion to his beautie; noe color vnremovd that may ſtaine his reputacon; but that his name, like his virtue ſhall be cleer; cleer from all ſtaines, all aſperſions, & all ieolouſies: cleer in y^r iudgment (ô Athenians): cleer in the iudgment & opinions of all good men. ffor the firſt that Socrates not anſwearinge, made a defeᶜtion from the law, in not conforming to the pp'ceſſe, wch is a rule propoſ'd to all men, and not to be declined, I might firſt ſay ther was noe ſuch thinge in faᶜt, and therefore noe deliᶜtion in that pointe; and this truth were moſt aparant. ffor noe pp'ceſs does require the exact p'formance of a thinge. that might impoſe an impoſsi- bilitie on the p'tie; as the payment of a ſumm to him

Page 27. that has it not; the ſatiſſaᶜtion of a mul[c]t/ layd by the wiſedome of ſome Judges beyond the p'portion of the fortune from whence it ſhould be iſsuinge, and the like; wch were an abſurditie in reaſon; & therefore noe lawe commaunds impoſsibilities: but a double way is beſt for the fulfillinge of that rule; the authoritie of the p'ceſse ſtandes in a dilemma; either this muſt be done, or that; either the thinge commanded, as the payment of the debt, the ſatiſſaccon of the mulᶜt, & the like; or a ſubmiſsion of the partie, a rendringe of ye perfon to the difcreation of the law, either of wch is a full anfwear to the p'cefse, and soe Socrates by his sufferance, & imprifonment made a expiation of that guilt & is free from that defeccon. But this reafon I intend not to infift on, as to[o] light an argument for Socr[ates] to[o] narrow for his caufe, wch muft have the full comp^{r}henfion of all law. & not reft/ on part nor be fupported by the formes, to become worthy of his innocence. Socrates has iuftice it selfe to warrant him, in his silence and retention : the generall authoritie of the law, to anfwear the p'ticular procefse made againft him as the Common right of Athens, y^r liberties ô Athenians, the p'vifions of y^r ffathers, the p'mulgations of y^r elders, all declaringe, all confirringe, all approveing that antient priviledge of Senate. wch Senat does entertaine the well-fare of this nacon ; & that priviledg the Senat. By this priviledg, wch is prov'd in the firft arguments of our Socrates, noe other Court has iurifdiccon in the bufinefse of that place, noe other Judg has cognifance of fuch caufes; if ther an offence be done (wch what credulitie can thinke an offence fhould ther be perpetrat wher all errors are reformed ?) if Socrates fhould offend in the agitacōns/ of that Counfell (and whoe cann once beleeve that Soc[rates] was offendinge ? who cann imagine his counfells should be faulty who had noe action, no intention not moft regular ?) if both Socrates and that Cõuncell fhould be faulty, faulty in high degree, faulty in any meafure, yett noe other Judg may queftion them ; noe other Court has authoritie to iudg them : they are exempt by the

Page 28.

Page 29.

p^rviledg of Senate, that sacred relique of antiquitie, y^t palladium of this Cittie; what offences are ther done, muſt ther likewiſe be complaind of; &, if they doe deſerve it, they muſt ther likewiſe be corrected. *ther, & noe wher elſe*, ſay thoſe reſolucõns of ould tyme wch formerly were noted: *ther, & not by them*, as thoſe iudges did confeſse it. *not in inferiour Courts*, as thoſe antient declaracõns/ did expreſſe it. But in the Senate muſt thoſe accõns of the Senat be determined, in that Counſell wch onely cann have knowledg of thoſe ſecretes, whoſe franchiſe & immunitie it is, (confeſt by all prioritie, & in all former practiſes exhibited) to be the only Judg vpon it ſelfe. & the reaſon is evident in this caſe, for ther is noe Court ſuperiour to the Senate, naie ther is none that's equall; none not inferior vnto that; & it is an axiome in the law, *par in parem non habet poteſtatem*; & if not an equall on an equall, much leſse an inferior cann have that power on his ſup'ior, wch is contrary to all laws, the lawes of man, the lawes of God, the lawes of nature: ffor (as the lawes of man have laid that ground & principle) the lawes of God confirme it, wch ſtill command obedience to ſup'iors, honor to elders; &/ the ſenate to all other Courtes, (wch noe man will denie) is both higher, & elder as the ſpring, & fountaine whence their originalls are deductit. to wch the lawes of nature correſpond, as wee have it in the qualitie of a Child, wch admitts noe power, or iuriſdiccõn on the ffather. Therefore noe other Court cann have y^t influence on the Senate, nor Juriſdiccõn on that priviledg, or on Socrates, as a Senator; but all law, all libertie, all right; all p^rſident, and example, all concefsion, and acknowledgment; of all perfons, in all tymes, give them a free exemption, naie, by that right, impofe a necefsitie on Socrates, not to fubmitt his caufe, wch were to fubmitt that right; & soe to make Socrates, by the counterchange of action, turne his innocence into guilt; & wher he nowe ftandes innocent, to become guiltie of this crime wch his traducers have obiected. wher then/ is that defection from the lawe, y^t great crime in Socrates? is it to have been conftant to that principle, not to decline that rule? · does it implie a difobedience to the former, that the matter, & fubftance is reteyn'd? is the p'ceffe neglected, wher the law it felf is followed, when an exact obfervance is p'form'd? cann the lefser challenge duty, & obedience contrary to the service and attendance wch is commanded by the greater? heer the greater did command Socrates not to anfwear, not to make fubmifsion of his caufe, the caufe & intereft of the Senat, y^r intereft ô Athenians, the right and title of y^r fathers & not the caufe of Socrates, but as he was a member of y^r body; the greater I say did command him not to anfwear, not to make fubmifsion of his caufe, to the lefse, to the inferior authoritie of the Judges, & soe not to obey their p'cesse. Therefore/ in this he made noe defection from the law, nor is faultie, & guiltie of that crime, in wch he ftands fufpected. ffor the fecond offence wch is suppofed againft our Socrates, the contempt of Juftice, in not submittinge to authoritie wher a iudgmen^t & sentence did require it; wher ther was a definition in the pointe, a refolucon given by the iudges of the lawes, that Socrates ought to anfwear; ther to be

Page 32.

Page 33.

silent, as tis said, makes Socrates to be refractary, renders him stubborne, & contemptuous againſt the formes of Juſtice. & this is vrged as a crime of higher nature, an offenc that's more tranfcendent (as a iudgmᵗ is held greater then a p'ceſs) and foe Socrates more faultie. to wᶜʰ though the fame anſwear might be made that was given vnto the other; & the defence were/ p'fect, and compleat in the same arguments, & reafons, yett we will deale more p'ticularly heerein to worke yᵉ cleerer fatiſfaccon, to vindicate the honor of our Socrates, to repell the whole fury of his enemyes, to leave noe color for their slanders, noe pʳiudice on his innocence. ffor this therefore wee will firſt, remove the fuppoficon they haue made, that a iudgment is greater then a p'ceſſe, & then their aggravation falls to ground: then we will shew that in not anfwearinge to that iudgmᵗ ther was noe contempt of Juſtice, yᵗ Socrates was not refraϾtary to Juſtice in not conforminge to thofe iudges; and for this wee will fetch our argumentes, partly from the caufe, partly from the confideracon of the p'fons, wᶜʰ will prove that Socrates was not faultie. ffor the suppoficon, that a iudgment is greater/ then a procefſe; that the denunciation of a Court is of more authoritie then the writt, take but this difference, this short diſtinϾtion to refute it. the procefſe is the authenticke aϾt ot'h law; the iudgment but the word, & sentence of a man. the writ is as the letter it self of Juſtice, the denunciation of a Court but the opinion of the iudges: whether then is greater, the authoritie of the law, or the word, & sentence of a man? the opinion of a iudge, or yᵉ letter it self of

Page 34.

Page 35.

iuftice? lett any man determine it, let the decifion be by them; by thofe enemyes of Socrates, vpon thofe groundes lett Socrates be iudg'd: nor appeale shall goe noe further in this cafe, then to their confciences. lett them now speake whether their aggravation be well laid. iudgments maie err, men may be deceav'd & many fallacies are incident to/ opinion: but the law, & Juftice are ftill certaine, Page 36. ther is noe variacon in their rules; therefore the sentence of the iudges cannot be more valid then the authoritie of the law. But to leav this and to anfwear the contempt, to shew that Socrates was not refractarie vnto Juftice, in not conforminge to ye opinion of the iudges; lett vs firft weigh the caufe, how in the p^{r}fent right it bound him, & then the confequence, what operacon, what effectes it might induce; weigh it as the publicke caufe of Athens, not the privat intereft of Socrates, as the right, & title of the Senat, not only as the queftion of our Socrates. & then it will appeer what contempt he has committed, & how farr Socrates is faultie. the caufe y^u know was the priviledge of the Senat. to the maintenance of y^t priviledg,/ befides Page 37. the Comon tye of all men, Socrates had a prop[er] obligacon, both for the truft comitted to him, & his p'ticular duty to that place. if then Socrates by conforminge to the iudges should have done any thing in p^{r}iudice of that priviledg, it muft have been a violacon of the generall, & p'ticular obligacon wch he had, & 'ʂoe a forfeit of his duty. now that the conforming to the iudges, had been a p^{r}iudice of that priviledg, as tis apparant in the refolucons, is moft 2. H. 4. pregnant in the Statutes, that were cited. wherein ther's 4. H. 8.

not only a declaracon of the right, but an iniunction laid on Soc[rates] that he shall not difcover the pafsages of ye Senat; & then he cannot anfwear to the queftion of thofe things when the anfwear muft difcouer them. this for the/ right, & the duty of our Socrates, the difcharge of wch admitts of noe contempt, for good & evill have noe competition; the confequence yett is of farr greater obfervacon; more prefsing in the pointe, more bindeing vpon Socrates: for by granting this, Socrates muft grant all; bye submittinge the p^riviledge in this cafe, he for his part muft submit it in all others; all bufinesse of the Senat he muft yeeld to the iurifdiccon of the iu[d]ges if he admit their authoritie, vpon this: all fecretts of that Counfell wch shalbe treafurd in his breaft, muft he open, if they haue this power, & influence on his person; for the queftion only gives intelligence of the fact, & before examinacon ther can be noe diftinccon made of the differenc of caufes; all fecretts and not fecretts are the fame before they are truly knowen, & ther is noe knowledg but by triall, wch triall makes an openinge and difcovery./ & thus all the secrets of the Senat wch were involved on Socrates muft be fubiect to the Judges; the moft intimate counfells of that conclave obnoxious to their cenfure. they wth the leaft p^rtenfe might queftion them; not takeing knowledge of their nature; & by that queftion Socrates muft difcover them; for what he had once admitted he could not afterwards retract, wth what effect might follow it, what operacon it would have, what danger to our Socrates, what danger to the Senat, what danger to this State, I referr it to your wifedome ô Athenians, when yr whole felicity & happinefse has dependance on that Counfell as the honor of our Socrates on integrite! can it be thought therefore a contempt in Socrates againft Juftice to have infifted on this priviledg? can it be thought a guilt not to fubmitt this right? cann Socrates be faultie, to haue p^rferv'd his duty to the Senat, his duty to his Country, the neglect whereof did threaten soe/ much danger vnto either? if this Page 40. be a contempt, lett all men then be guilty; to p^rferve the publicke right, to fupport the common fafetie, lett all men, foe, be guiltie of contempt. but further if ther had not been this necefsitie of priviledg; if nothing but ye importance, as 'twas the caufe ot'h Senat, had been obvious vnto Socrates, could Socrates wth the fafety of his iudgm^t have fubmitted it to Melitus, he who had said, who had said publickly to Socrates, by way of overture in that Court, that the Senat had noe priviledg, that it had noe power of iudicature, that it only could make lawes, & had noe proceedings but that way, noe power of execucon? could Socrates, wth the fafety of his iudgment, have made fubmifsion of that right to him that soe litle vnderftood it? Socrates/ could not fubmitt the caufe ot'h senate, to such Page 41. iudges, wch were not fitt to have been iudges vpon Socrates. wch reafon of ye p'fons, if noe other were obiected, were in this caufe sufficient to excufe him, & to acquitt Socrates of that guilt. To defcend then to the next, the next offence of Socrates, wch is fuggefted in his charge, that Socrates in not anfwearinge did defert the p'teccon of his innocence & expof'd himfelf to fcandall, by y^t filence, & retention;

litle on this will serve to avoid yᵉ accufaccon. ffor firſt in generall his innocence is confeſt ; & what more is needfull for the iuſtification of oʳ Socrates ? what guilt cann be fufpected wher his innocence is acknowledg'd ? if he be innocent, how cann he then be faultie ? if faultie how cann he then be innocent ? the truth in this was to[o] fubtile for his adverfaries, even through their mallice sallying to defend him ; what they intended for a charge, muſt be an ap[o]logie for Socrates,/ what they obiected as a crime, muſt be a pointe of meritt. ô truth, great is the wonder of thy virtue, even aboue all things thou art ſtrong; becaufe Socra[tes] did follow thee, thou wilt follow Socrates: becaufe he was thy fervant, thou haſt foe commanded it, that his enemies ſhould ferve him ; & this falls in the generall confefsion of his innocence ; but in p'ticular in this act of Socrates, or rather this neglect wᶜʰ is pʳtended in his caufe, that Socrates not anfwearing made a defertion of his innocence, confider firſt what that innocence imports, & then meafure it by the fact : yᵘ ſhall ther finde, not an innocence deferted, but moſt religiouſly maintained : Socrates suffering for his innocence, not doeing any lying to impeach it, Socrates in his blood writting thefe Characters for pofteritie, not expofing his vertue vnto fcandall. This yᵘ ſhall fee if yᵘ confider but that principle, what that innocence importes, and then/ applie it to the fact, therein you shall finde that Socrates is not guiltie. Innocence is not the opinion of the many, the reputacon of one act, the freedome from some guilt, but a generall virtue and integretie, a fpotlefse faultlefse courfe, in the faithfull execution of all duties, the difcharge, and p'formance of all offices, in wch the greater ftill muft be preferrd before the lefse. now in this duty of o^r Socrates wher the publicke intereft was in queftion, noe peculiar, noe private faculties of his owne, might be brought in competition, if the reputacon of o^r Socrates had depended on that act. wher the publicke right ot'h Senat was in counterpoife, the fcales muft not be turn'd to the honor of o^r Socrates againft ye publicke & greater interefts, of the Senat; nor could it be a preiudice to his virtue to move, *in ordine*, to the publicke. Socrates was bound to prefer that greater right, his virtue did/ oblidge him to the obfervance of y^t duty, it was the innocence of Socrates not to decline this office; not to decline the publicke good, for the advantage of his private; this will iuftifie o^r Socrates if it be truly weighed againft the ftrength of all oppofers. But p'chance it wilbe faid, all men are not capable of this; all men have not the apprehenfion of this duty; but all men know the informacon that was made, the ftrange crimination againft Socrates; & Socrates in their iudgment makes himself guilty of them all, by refufing of his anfweare, & soe deferts his innocence.

To this I muft reply that though all this were true, yett it were noe reafon for the condemnacon of o^r Socrates, for if all men should soe thinke, that Socrates were not innocent, yet it must not move his virtue, rather to feem, then be: it muft not be a fatiffaccon vnto Socrates, that men doe thinke him innocent, Socr[ates] muft be soe,/ what ever men doe thinke him. heaven and his confciens muft give teftimonie for Socrates, thofe two muft iuftifie his innocence, though all the world condemne it. But heer is noe such thing in fact that Socrates is soe doubted, Socrates is not obnoxious to that danger in the true ſtate ot'h cauſe; for as all men know how Socrates was charged, all men knew the reaſon why Socrates did not anſwear; that it was for fear ot'h publicke priviledg & preiudice, not in ieloufie of himſelfe: that Socrates expoſ'd his fortune, and his p'ſon to p'ſerve the right ot'h Senat; that Socrates prized his ſafety, not as the liberties of Athens; that his life was not soe tender as his innocence: therefore that reason will not maintaine the charge, wch moſt vniuſtly is ſoe laid, to accuſe him as forſakinge what by all ſtuddie, & indeavour; by expoſing of his fortune, by expoſeing of his p'ſon, by his liberty, by his life, he laboured to preſerve./

Page 46. could ther be greater innocence then heerin Socrates did expreſſe? cann ther be such an argument for Socrates as this innocence of his? they were enough to anſwear all accuſers, all crimes, all charges, all obiections: herein Socrates might ſtop the mouth of all detraction, & give full ſatiſfaccon of his innocence; an innocence, for the admiracon of all others, the imitation of the Athenians: Socrates may yett glorie in the act, & triumph on his enemyes: he hath by this one virtue, by this ſole innocence overcome them. But yett they doe impute another crime to Socrates & faylinge in the reſt they would make him traitor to y^r liberties, to y^u ô Athenians, they would make Socrates an enemy, in y^r right & priviledg they would render him a traitor. what he was moſt affective to conſerve that they would make him moſt effective to deſtroy. in not conſenting to the iuriſdiccon of the iudges, they doe ſuppoſe him guiltie of enlarging/ their authoritie; by denying it in one thinge to give it them in all; to force them to aſsume it in the p'ticular of his cauſe, & by that aſsumption to creat a p^{r}ſedent for the generall. this charge is many waies unproved, & by varietie of inſtrument. thoſe that are his enemies delate it to divide him from y^r favours: thoſe that were his iudges vſe it in extenuacon of their sentence; his accusers, his informers, & a generacon worſe then theſe, his ſeeminge frendes, & ſociats, who p^{r}tend nothing but zeale, in the publicke cauſe, & intereſt, but intend only their privat avarice and corruptions; theſe all, but, moſt of all, theſe laſt, diffuſe this ſcandall againſt Socrates, & to cover their envie vnto him vſe the ptext & color of affection to y^r ſervice. to theſe ſome thing muſt be ſaid in apologie for Socrates, ſomethinge to p^{r}ſerve him from y^r priudice & diſlike; not that their reaſons doe deſerve it, that it is vrg'd by the weight & preſsure/ of their charge, but that his virtue does require it, that ther be noe place lefte to Scandall, that ther be noe reſidenc for detraccon vpon the accõns of o^r Socrates: that, as his perſon, his fame likewiſe may be innocent. ffirſt therefore to ſhew that the iudges were not vrg'd to aſsume that iuriſdiccon vpon Socrates, but that their act was voluntarie, & not neceſsitated & enforc't, wee muſt a litle recapitulat the order of that cauſe. Socrates being charg'd for matter done in Senate pleades the priviledg of that Counſell, & therefore proves his cauſe not ſubiect to their cogniſance. The Judges make

Page 47.

Page 48.

a refolucon againft this, & determine vpon Socrates, that their is noe fuch right it'h Senat, noe such priviledg for him. soe as in this they made a decifsion of that queftion & conclufion of that right, wthout the help of Socrates, naie contrary to his labour, & afsum'd that iurifdiccon to themfelves: soe that what followes was but the confequent/ of this; the iudgment given on Socrates, but an effect of that preiudice to the Senat. the priviledg being denied in their firft act, that afsumption was their owne; for the next was meerly the fingle cause of Socrates, wherein the fact only was confiderable, the right wholy beinge determined in the former; and therein Socrates was not guiltie of necefsitating their iudgment, but that p^{r}iudice was meerly of themfelves, a voluntary afsumption in that cafe, an effected entrance & invafion of the priviledg of the Senat.

But if it had been otherwife, that Socr[ates] enforct them by fome necefsitie to this act (wch who cann thinke that Socrates would doe, whofe doeing & fufferring had soe contrary an intention by his pleading?) at the firft indeavoring to p^{r}vent it; by his not pleading at the laft giveing a newe occafion, (for whereas by anfwearing he had reduc't their iudgment to the matter, wherein ftill the priviledg was involv'd,/ by not anfwearing he brought it to his p^{r}fon, soe as therein it was only a iudgm^t vpon Socrates wch otherwife would have been a new conclufion vpon the priviledg) & therefore who cann thinke that Socrates, both doeing and suffering to that end, should soe enforce them to the p^{r}iudice of this priviledg? But if it had been soe, if by suppoſicon we admitt it, does that p'ticular conclude generally for all others? will that inſtance againſt Socrates creat a p'fect right it'h Judges? examples are noe rules; noe errors their examples, but what becomes a p'ſident muſt have both vſe, & right; right, for the foundacon, & originall; & vſe to ſhew the ſup'ſtruccon & contynuance *non firmatur tractu temporis*, ſay their ould lawiers, *quod de iure ab initio non ſubſiſtit*, & as the new, *all right has being & ſubſiſtenc by vſe and acceptacon*, therefore though Socrates had enforc't that accon on the iudges, that act would not conclude their iuriſdiccon on all others, nor could Socrates therein be/ guiltie of that crime of betrayinge of y^r liberties, nor wthout impietie may be thought, as was ſuggeſted in the charge, a traitor to himſelfe, a traitor to the Senat, a traitor to his Country. y^u have heard how much he did to p'ſerve the publicke intereſtes; y^u know how much he ſuffered to p'ſerve his innocence therein; ſhould I enumerat his paſsions I should renewe y^r greifes; inſtead of cureinge Socrates, I should wound yu ô Athenians I should peirce the soule of y^r affections wth the memory of y^r Socrates, the memorie of his virtues, the memorie of his meritt, his pietie and integritie to y^u, his ſenceritie & fidelitie to the Senat, his love and charitie to all; in all beyond all meaſure of compariſon, vnmatcht, vnparalel'd, vnexampled; to renew the memorie of theſe virtues I should renew the affection of y^r loſses & turne this apologie for Socrates into a Common Elege of the Athenians. I will not therefore/ by the comm[em]eracon of his virtues cauſe the renovacon of y^r greifes, and as I paſse his merits,

Page 51.

Page 52.

soe I will doe his sufferings, I will not enumerat his pafsions to tell y^u what he suffered; what he suffer'd in his ffortune, what he suffered in his perfon, in his liberty, in his life: to be made poore & naked; to be imprifoned and reftrain'd; nay not to be at all; not to hav[e] the proper vfe of any thinge, not to have knowledg of Societie; not to have beinge & exiftence: his faculties confifcat; his frendes debarr'd his prefence; himfelfe deprived the world: I will not tell y^u of all this suffer'd by yr Socrates; all this sufferd for yr service, for you moft excellent Athenians, for y^r Children, yr pofteritie, to p^rferve y^r rights and liberties; that as they were the inheritanc[e] of y^r fathers, from y^u likewife, they may againe devolve to them, I will not revive this memorie of his pafsions for your service, leaft in them, I should revive y^r memory/ of yor lofses, y^r lofses in yr Socrates, for whom y^r iuftice, not yr sorrow now I craue, to p^rtect him from his enemyes, to p^rtect him in his innocence, that vnmatcht innocence of Socrates againft their fcandalls, and detractions, to determine vpon the accufations y^u have heard, whether Socrates be guiltie, guiltie as is suggefted, of defeccon from the law, contempt of authoritie, & iustice, defertion of his owne innocence, betraying of yr liberties, in all wch as Socr[ates] was charg'd, for Socrates we have anfweared, what I hope will satiffie yor wifedomes, that Socrates was not faulty, for whom I crave y^r iudgments, as y^r pardon for my selfe.

*** A blank leaf follows. On *verfo* in Eliot's writing is ' Defence for Socrates.'—G.

II.
NEGOTIUM POSTERORUM

OR

SIR JOHN ELIOT'S

MEMORIALS

OF

THE PROCEEDINGS IN THE HOUSE OF COMMONS

DURING

THE FIRST PARLIAMENT AT LONDON

AND OXFORD

OF

CHARLES IST.

ETC. ETC. ETC.

NOTE.

See our Introduction for a defcription of the holograph MS. of the prefent remarkable work of Sir John Eliot; than which few more hiftorically valuable have been preferved. In an Appendix other Eliot MSS. at Port Eliot have been for the firft time utilized, to fupplement and illuftrate.—G.

NEGOTIUM POSTERORUM.

TRANGERS have obferved the felicities of England by hir Parliam[ts]. that & the contrary, is apparant in the examples of hir kings; of whom [thofe] whofe actions had concurrence wth that Councell, were alwaies happie & succesfull; thofe that contefted or neglected it, unprosperous & vnfortunat. of the firft forte in the old times, were thofe victorious & brave princes E[dward] 1. E[dward] 3. H[enry] 5., that soe farr extended the honor of their nation in the admiration of all others, as even the name of Englifhmen could doe wonders of it felf, taking & giving kingdomes as the fubjects of their wills. of the latter, were thofe characters of misfortune E[dward] 2, R[ichard] 2. H[enry] 6., whofe raignes were all inglorious & diftracted [&] fatall [in] their Ends. but above all, for a demonftration in this pointe, is that inftance before thefe, of H[enry] 3; who in his younger times/ affecting the fals reafons of his favorits, in opposition of the parl involved his crowne & Kingdome in fuch miferie & dif-

F

honors, as few times els can paralell. princes have seldome sufferd; but vpon the apprehension of those errors, & retracting of that course in his reconciliation & coniunction w^h that great counsell of his people (those flies of Court reiected) he againe recoverd the lost honor vnto both, restord their antient happiness, livd & enioyed it in a sweet calmeness & tranquilitie, & dying left it as an inheritance to his sonne, who on that ground directed the superstructure of his greatness. H[enry] 4. E[dward] 4. H[enry] 7. who raisd their ffortunes by the falls of those before them, made their errors their instructions, & by complying w^h the parl. what they had gott w^h hasard, w^h securitie they retaynd./ H[enry] 8. though otherwise rough & violent, did nothing in preiudice of that Court, or if it were attempted in some perticular by his ministers, (as the most righteous times are not without obliquities) it was soone retracted by himselfe, who maintained his confidence wth his people; & he was not without reputation w^h his neighbours, nor this nation in dishonor vnder him. that hopefull prince his sonne E[dward] 6. in the short time he livd, having the same affiance, lessened not in the expectation of the world. but that glorious starr, his sister, of most ever-famous memorie Q[ueen] El[isabeth] (for thother is not observable on this part either for hir cuncelles or successes, hir marriage & alliance leading contrary). that princess who was glorious above all,—all that went before her,—in whom all their vertues & soe their honors were contracted, (for the sweetness & pietie of hir brother; the magnanimitie of hir ffather; the

Page 3.

wifdome of hir grandfather; the ffortune &/ valor of the Page 4.
reft, were all compleat in hir, whom Mars & Apollo did
present for a wonder to the world); this excellent Minerva
was the daughter of that Metis, that great Councell of the
parl. was the nurse of all hir actions; & fuch an Emulation was of Love between that Senat & this Q [ueen], as
it is questionable whether had more affection, the parl. in
obfervance vnto hir, or she in indulgence to the parl.
what were the effects of this hir ftories do delineat : peace
& prosperitie at home, honor & reputation abroad ; a love
& obfervation in hir friends, confternation in hir enemyes,
admiration even in all; the Ambitious pride of Spaine
broken by hir powers; the diftracted ffrench revnited by
hir artes; the diftreft Hollanders supported by hir succors;
the seditious Sc[otch] reduc'd to the obedience of their
prince; all violence & iniurie repeld; all vsurpation &/
oppression counter-wrought; the weake assisted; the Page 5.
necessitous releivd; men & monie into divers parts sent
out, as if England had beene the magazine of them all, &
she the Queftor that had the dispenfation of these treafures;
or rather the Pretor & Judge of all their controverfies.
who wth this magnificence abroad did not impaire at home,
but being good to all, was moft iuft & pious to hir fub-
iects; who by a free possession of their liberties, increafed
in wealth & plentie, & not wthstanding that infinite of
expence for support of all thofe charges, the riches of hir
checker did improve.

this fhewes the importance of the parl^s & the happinefs
of the State; & how all the Engl[ifh] Kings have beene

fortunat by that Councell, none without it. therfore in the description of the parl. wilbe beft seene the state & condition of the Kingdome: in that wilbe emergent/ the difeafes wch it suffers; sometimes propounded in their fervor or extremitie for a present cure & help; sometimes in the inclination & beginning, before they are come to heigth for the prevention of the danger; sometimes by way of prophecie discovered as they are but in Embrione & conception; both their originalls & degrees come often, ther mob agitation & debate, alwaies their acts & confequences, & now & then their reafons. I speak thus of their reafons becaufe it is not alwaies that the true caufe is feene. the fame effect may flow from divers principles & intentions. often w^h ftates & men *aliud pretenditur, aliud in mente eft;* ther are as the civilians have obfervd *caufæ fuaforiæ, caufæ iuftificæ,* & both concurring in great actions; for w^{ch}/ dissimulation is defined to be *politiæ particulæ imago,* & this makes thefe reafons more obfcure, wch yet in parl come sometimes to discussion; wher thofe mifteries & secrets are vnlockt; & as the dangers, soe the fafties are ther treated of, w^h all their incidents & concommitants, connexions, adiunctions, & dependancies; what in religion, or abilitie has relation to the Kingdome, the knowledge of it moves in the agitations of the parl wch agitations therfore wilbe a good mirror of the times. ffor this, however inglorious it may feeme, I have dispofd my thoughts in the service of my Countrie, to compose the ftorie of that Councell from the end of Q[ueen] El[isabeth]. what was the condition of the kingdome when hir government did

leave it, is well knowne to all men; what it is now, this
Labor will express,/ & somewhat of the reason, as it is in- Page 8.
finuated by the acts wilbe emergent in this worke, not els
wher soe discernable, if either my penne or prospect doe
not faile me. manie will thinke (& that perhaps not
lightly) the scope of this too narrow, for a hiftorie; but
Wee that take it otherwife, defire their favor in our
Cenfure, vntill they againe confider it: Let them pervfe
the passages, obferve the varietie of ther treaties, note ther
resolutions & effects, read & digest them, & then infer
the iudgment; in wch we are confident they will finde
somewhat of delight, & the reft not much vnprofitable.

But before we imbarque in this storie of the parl^s it will
not be vnnecessarie, in our waie to take some short survey
of that bodie; how it is composd [&] by what authoritie
it subfifts: for noe little preiudice may be done it, in the
opinion it receaves *modo habendi*/ for the accession of hir Page 9.
powers, what ever act & exercife it have had. if it be new
by concession of late times, the times that change their
reafons may have some color likewife to change the refolu-
tion of that grant: if the continuance have beene longer, &
yet the grant appeers, (though it be much to impeach the
prescription of a kingdome wch for manie ages recites [pre-
cedents], one being admitted for the privat interestes of men)
it may be some pretext that the favor of one prince should
not conclude the generation of succefsors: but if the
inftitution be more antient & without the introduction of
such grant; or that that grant of one be still confirmed by
all, then all are in the faith & obligation, & the authoritie

of that counfell is much more, as it subfifts by right & not by favor.

Page 10. I know the vulgar & common tradition/ does refute that parl^s. had beginning wth thofe charters wch were made by H[enry] 3. & that he that granted thofe liberties to the people gave being vnto parl^s. vpon wch foundation many arguments are laid to impaire the worth of either ; the weakness of that king, the greatness of his barons, the tumults of that time, wch made a necessitie of thofe grantes that were not taken, but extorted : but truth shall speake for both, how iniurious is this slander ; how much more antient & authentick their defcent.

NEGOTIUM POSTERORUM.

TOMUS SECUNDUS, LIBER PRIMUS.

NEGOTIUM POSTERORUM.

[ING] J[AMES] being dead & wth him the fearfull securitie & degenerat vices of a long corrupted peace in hope & expectation laid aside, wth the new K[ing] a new spirit of life & comfort possest all men, as if the ould Genius of the kingdome, having wth Endimion slept an age, were now awak't againe, moving in all the partes & members of the bodie, to the quickening & agitation of the whole. the blood wch was the vehicle of this spirit, by divers veines was carried from the ffountaine of those hopes, the virtues of K[ing] C[harles], to that sea of Love & dutie in the harts & affections of the people. in some the consideration of his pietie, his religious practise & devotion, his choise & conftant preservation of that iewell in the mids't of those prestigious artes of Spaine, & his publick professions, being from thence returnd, did cause that ioye & hope : others were movd by the innate sweetnes of his nature, the calme habit & composition of his minde : his exact goverment in the œconomie, the order of his house, the rule of

his affaires, the disposition of his servantes, being Prince, all in a great care, & providence, to the/ expression of his honor, & yet noe thrift neglected, of w^{ch}, besides the order & direction, he was an example in himself: his publicke industrie, & studies to improve his knowledg in the State, & to advance that business, were an indication vnto others. his diligence & attendance at all Councells, forwardness in all business wch might render satiffaction to the subiectes, as the much long'd for dissolution of those treaties, the vntying of those knotts, the cutting of those Gordian yokes in wch they were held by Spaine & the preparations thervpon for revenge of all their iniuries, & reparation of his frindes, wch works were taken for a present of his virtue & a promise for the future of greater hopes to come: his exercise & recreations were not left [out] but some deduc'd their reasons ev'n from them, both for his choife & temper; & all having in somethinges their perswasion, some in all thinges to whom the change alone seem'd fortunat, & this againe indeard by reflection on the contraries; when it was thought what infelicities had béene sufferd, infelicities abroad, infelicities at home, in the consumption of the honor, consumption of the treasures of the kingdome; the martiall powers neglected, the reputation of their wisdome in contempt,/ Mars & Apollo forsaking them in that inextricable laborinth of those treaties, whereby religion was corrupted, iuftice perverted; & all this through facilitie & confidence, or a toomuch Love of peace: the change wch was now presumed in these, by the new change of persons wrought a new change of harts; all mens affections were transferd from doubt & ielosie into hope, & all their fears & sorrows did resolve themselves to ioye. ffor confirmation of all these, as that wch was to be the assurance of them all, & of all els that might import the happinefs of the kingdome, a Parliament was intimated. the Summons & formalities dispatch't, the obiections of the Commons being prepar'd wth more then vsual diligenc, the emulation for the service being greater : the members chosen forthwth repair'd to London to make their attendance at the time; noe man would be wanting : Love & ambition gave them wings; he that was firft seem'd happieft; zeale & affection did so worke, as that circumstance was thought an advantage in the dutie. To heighten the celebration of this meeting, the Q[ueen] was then expected/ out of ffrance. The desposorio's being past & the Ambassadors wth their new mistris on their iorney, the roiall navie did attend hir transportation on the Seas. the K[ing] himself past downe to Canterburie to receave hir, wher the enterviewe & nuptialls being perform'd in a state answearable to their worths, they made their repaire to London, & in that firft coniunction begott both Love and admiration. this defer'd awhile the openinge of the Parliament, (but the feftivitie of the time, was a compensation for that want,) wch by prorogation was continued vntill the eighteenth daie of June, all men in the meane time being full of ioy and comfort, when, as a Crowne to all, that Solemnitie was added.

Page 4.

To the first ceremonies & entrance the D[uke] of Chevr'es & his Ladie were admitted, wth the Ambassadors & others of the ffrench, who in honor & attendance of the

Q[ueen], had accompanied hir from ffrance. a place they had in the Lords house belowe the corner of the State, the Q[ueen] being likewise present, all the Lords in their formalities & orders, & the Commons in great ioye & expec-/ tation, when the K[ing] applying his speech vnto the time, & both the time & that vnto himself, thus gives a short character of either, & in that renders the occasion of the assembly.

My Lords & gentlemen, my naturall disabilitie to speake houlds good correspondence wth this time wch being designd for action, discourses will not fit it; nor is it needfull in the business of this meetinge that my exhortations should be long, it being begunne before, in my ffathers daies, when both I & you were severallie ingag'd, I as y^r intercessor vnto him, y^u by y^r advise & declaration for the worke; it would be now a dishonor to vs both not to give it perfection by our help & such supplie of necessaries as the importance does require. I speake not this in diffidence of y^r readiness, but as an expresion of my sence vpon the publick interest. I know y^r Zeale & affection to religion, & that matchless fidelitie to y^r K[ing] wch is the antient honor of this nation. for my part I seeke nothing/ for my self but in the common happinefs, for wch I shalbe as readie to dispose my privat faculties, as I doubt not of y^r willingness to ayd me; by wch concurrence both power & reputation wilbe gainde, & a presage & prediction to our hopes.

both the sence & shortness of this expression were well Likt, as meeting wth the inclination of the time, wch wearied wth the long orations of K[ing] J[ames] that did inherit but the winde, was much mov'd at this brevitie & plainness, more like to truth then art, that it drew a great applause to follow it, answearable to the opinion wch it wrought, that wth the manners of their Ancestors, they should resume their ffortunes, & in this turne & revolution, meet the ould world againe. Some time being given, vpon the conclusion of this speech, as the State & admiration did require, the B^p of Lincolne then Lo. Keeper, taking his directions from the K[ing] thus seconds him, in more words, but as a paraphrase onlie on that text.

My Lords & gentlemen, y^u have heard his Maties speech, of wch I may say, as of the like it was, that ther/ was *multum in parvo*, & though it contain'd somuch as ther is little lefte for me, yet it deserves that censure wch Plinie gives of Homer, vpon the aboundant expression of his works, that ther was noe word in vaine. all was said in that word of the ingagement wch concern'd the business of this time: for vpon that ingagement of the Last Parliament to K[ing] J[ames] he was induc'd to dissolve the treaties then wth Spaine; that necessarily did enforce him to a warr; for the warr ther must be varietie of preparation; to that end he contracted a league wth other princes, added some forces to the States, levied an armie for Count Manffeilt, arm'd his owne ships for Sea, & of them provides a navie, wch now we may call invincible, in all to scatter the forces of his enemies in the whole circumference of their dominions, by wch he became

Page 7.

ingag'd to the expectation of the world, & as a legacie by his bequest & y^{rs} left that ingagement to his Sonne, who now desires to/ follow it for y^r honors & his owne. in the preparations that are past, all the subsidies & fifteenths wch formerlie y^u haue given, are spent, & much more of the revenew, for wch now y^r further ayd is crav'd & wthout wch the work cannot proceed, wherin three circumstances onlie I will add.

the first for time, wch is the great commander in all actions; for actions command not time, but time them, & therfor that supplie that comes too late proves noe supplie at all. Europe is now ſtir'd like the poole of Bethesda by the Angell, for the recoverie of the honor & happiness of this nation, & if we slip the opportunitie, some other may prevent vs; wherfor it is desir'd we should give this meeting to this business. the second circumstance is the manner, wch time does vse in action, as the wings about hir feet, wherin if y^u finde the vsuall waie too slacke, fear not in an occasion of such consequence to resort to others fitter. all are subventions wch are granted by this bodie, nor can it be vnparliamentary/ wch is resolv'd by Parliament. the third circumstance & last, is the end & issue of this action, wch carries wth it the ffame & reputation of our K[ing]. for as princes sowe in actions, soe they shall reap in glorie, & the hope & glorie of our Soveraigne (wch is all that kings possess) he has now putt on vs, not, in desperation, as Cæsar wth the Romans *iacta est alea :* but in confidence as his owne motto has it, *amor civium regis munimentum*. Kings and subiects *relata simul sunt natura*, as the Civilians have observ'd, & noe sooner shall his Matie be knowne a victorious prince, but y^u shalbe esteemd a valiant faithfull people. & soe to address y^n to this worke, y^u are now to chuse a Speaker & on tewfday next to present him to his Matie.

this ceremonie being ended, the Commons, according to the direction that was given, retir'd to their house for the election of their Speaker, wher a proposition being made by some privie Councellors of the K[ing], members of that house, for Sarient/ Crew, it was foorthw^th by the rest & after some formalities vsuall more then necessary of pretended vnwillingness in him, & importunitie in the others, wth much art & rhetoricke on both sides, he was led into the chaire, wch in obedience he assum'd, not yet in acceptation as his right. the nomination of this man was held a good omen to the worke. his former carriage in that place & the success therof after somanie nullities, & breaches, making againe as twere a new marriage & coniunction betweene the K[ing] & people, gaue such satisfaction in all hope, as all men were affected wth the choise. nor wanted ther in him either fitness or abilitie. he was a great master of the Lawe, & in his studies, religion had a share to a great name & reputation. his life & practice answear'd it. & his elocution was most apt for the imploiment he sustain'd ; for he could express him self on all occasions of the time *pulchre & ornate* as Quintilian makes his orator, *pro dignitate rerum, ad vtilitatem temporum, cum voluptate audientium*, nature &

art concurring to make him equall to the place; who vpon twefdaie after being p^rsented/ to the K[ing] & ther making an apologie for himself, wth a praier to be excusd, but not granted or allowd of, he thus submits to the burden of the service, & as his first fruits offerd vp this oration.

Since it is y^r Maties pleasure to command, it is my dutie to obey

——————— *tuum ô Rex magne quod optes explorare labor, mihi iussa capessere fas est.*

I know a sparrow falls not to the ground w^thout god's providence, &, as the rivers of waters, soe the harts of kings are in his hands, *impellit quo voluerit;* & I am the more incouraged by the former experience of the mercie & goodness of god, who at our last meeting, made those of one house to be of one minde, & united the head & members of one bodie in one hart, wch produced that *Parliamentum fœlix,* crowning wth honor, the memorie of the last publick act of y^r dear ffather to all posteritie, who then was pleased to aske & follow the advise of his great Councell in dissolving the two treaties; parted w^th/ some fruitfull leaves from the florishing garland of his Crowne, for the ease & benefit of his subiects, & gaue his roiall assent to as manie good lawes as past at anie one time since the Great Charter, in wch we then discernd y^r princelie care of the publicke, y^r readiness to remove all rubbs that might hinder, & y^r hand allwaies at hand to helpe & further our desires, & *beneficium postulat officium.*

And now that God hath put into y^r hart in y^r happie entrance to tread the true path of a Parliamentary waie, in comparison wherof all other courses are out of the waie, y^u have to y^r owne honor & our comfort shaken hands wth y^r subiects, & made y^r face to shine in the eyes of yr people. Solomon, the wisest of Kings, calls that land blessed whose K[ing] is the sonne of Nobles; & blessed are those subiects whose soveraigne trained vp in true religion, & by lineall defcent of inheritance, the vndoubted heir of the crowne; in the prime of his strength is invested in his roiall birthright by an immediat patent/ from God wth the applauses of his people. it is God's method wth his dearest children to mixe crosses wth comforts: but as a woman in travell forgets hir sorrowes for ioye that a man child is borne, soe o^r greife occasion'd by the departure of our late Soveraigne is swallowed vp wth ioye to see vpon his sun-sett, his owne sonne arising to succeed him, of whose happie & religious raigne & goverment we have a great expectation. God in his eternall councell had set the bounds of y^r ffather's daies, wch he could not pass, & the great hufbandman best knew the time when his corne was ripe, & readie to be gatherd into his granarj. it is he that made y^u, wch were, as yesterday our hopefull prince & the pledge of our future peace, to become our Soveraigne Lord & K[ing] & set y^u on yr ffather's throne to iudge the Israel of God. the good Hezekiah was 25 years ould when he begann to raigne, & soe now writes y^r Matie.

Page 13.

Page 14.

he did [walk] vprightlie in the sight of the Lord, sanctified the house of God, had in hart to make/ a Covenant wth the Lord; & God magnified him in the sight of all nations, & in euerie danger gave him deliverance; & y^r Matie shall become mightie wth Jotham while y^u direct y^r waie before the Lord yr God; y^u haue a faithfull & loyall people, that fear & love y^u, & *amor civium regis munimentum.* y^u haue a wise & vnderstanding Councell to advise; y^r imperiall diadem shines the brighter in that it is inamel'd & compast wth a bewtifull border of the antient & fundamentall lawes of this kingdome, wch as synewes, hould the bodie of the Common wealth together, & are suitable to the nature of the people, & safeſt for the Soveraigne. the Arke of true religion is wth y^u to waft y^u over the waters of all the dangers of this life, &, when y^u are ould & full of daies, to land y^u in the safe harbor of heaven. David being to goe the waie of all the world, gave a charge to Solomon his sonne to walke in the waies of God, that he might prosper in all he did; & it is our singular comfortes to hear that it was the

Page 15.

advise/ of yr dear ffather to y^u at his dying, to mayntaine the religion professed. in this we have long inioyd the blessing of peace, & gone foorth in the dance of them that be ioyfull. in this is the truth & power of God, the other a mist of man's invention, & a misterie of iniquitie. God whom we worship according to his word, bowing downe his ears to our ernest praiers, brought y^u back from forraigne parts, in a rare

adventure, full of perill, delivered y^u from the dangers
of the deepe, covered y^u vnder the wings of his immediat protection, suffred noe man to doe y^u harme,
& wrought a marvelous light out of a fearfull dark-
ness, worthie to be written wth a penne of iron &
pointe of a diamond in all true English harts. we
then for sorrow hangd o^r harpes vpon the willowes,
& could not singe the songs of Syon while y^u were in
a strange land. it is lodgd in the register of God's
speciall mercies to this nation, & y^r Matie may heerafter say

———— forsan et hæc olim meminisse ivabit/

y^r Matie hath the memorie of the distressed Pallitinat, Page 16.
wch in our distress in the times of persecution was a
sanctuarie & asylum, & everie good hart is sensible of
the dishonor to our nation to see & suffer a confederat
prince of our owne religion, an immediat match wth a
branch of the roiall blood, invaded & deforced of his
antient patrimonie & inheritance in that time when
ther was treatie of peace, & when our roiall navie
floted on forraigne seas & was to others a wall of brass
& tower of defence. Now that the scepter & sword
is come into y^r owne hands, extend it to hould vp
them that be helpless, that soe y^u may be a happie instrument to close vp the breaches, & raise vp the ruines
of that desolat countrie. qui non *propellit iniuriam
cum possit,!facit.* Egypt was destroied for being a staffe
of reed to the house of Israell ; & Meros was cursed

NEGOTIUM POSTERORUM.

Page 17.

for not comming to help the Lord in battaile against the mightie. Lucius a Brittanie K[ing] was the first of all Europe whose roiall/ diadem was brightned wth the heavenlie beames of christianitie; & y^u that are *rex totius Britanniæ*, liniallie defcended from the roiall stemme of both roses, & in whose person is an vnion of both kingdomes, shall add happinefs to yr crowne & state, by pulling downe the pride of that Antichristian Hierarchie, & in abandoning by publick edict, reallie executed, that wicked generation of Jesuites & Seminarie preistes, who are the sonns of Bichrie that blow the coales of contention, incendiaries that lie in waite to fett combustion; blood & powder are the badges of their wicked profession. y^r Matie noe doubt in y^r deepe wisdome doth discerne them, & in due time will curbe them, & noe longer suffer such Locusts to eat vp the good fruits of the Land, & to abuse the simple, least the church & commonwealth suffer, but send them home to their owne cells not to returne againe. But that I may not take away time, that is soe pretious, especiallie at this time, from y^r Maties/

Page 18.

soe manie & weightie affaires, nor hinder publicke business, I hasten to conclusion, & according to the dutie of my place, by speciall charge & commission from the Commons house, wth the warrant of antient & appr•ved presidents, I humblie present vnto y^r Matie our wonted & accustomed petitions.

1 that y^u would gratiouslie give allowance of our antient immunitie for our selves & such servants &

attendants as are capable of this priviledg, both *eundo et redeundo*, & during the time of our sitting, to be free from arrestes & troubles, whereby we may the better attend the publicke service.

2 that yr Matie would vouchsafe vnto vs libertie of free speech, according to our antient priviledg, that by a free debate of the reasons on both sides, truth may the better be discerned, & matters at last by common consent happilie concluded. & I doubt not but we shall confine our selves w^{th}in the limits & compass of dutie & obedience.

3 in regard/ the subiect may be such & of soe great moment & consequence, as shall minister iust cause of immediat resort for advise & redress, to the oracle of your owne mouth ; that y^r Matie would be pleased vpon all needfull occasions, vpon our humble suite, & at y^r fitt tyme, to permitt vs access to y^r roiall presence.

4 Laftlie, that y^r Matie would be gratiouslie pleased to entertaine vs in y^r gratious & good opinion & of all our proceedinges to make a benigne interpretation.

Ther onlie remaynes that I wch by the free choise of the house, & y^r Maties gratious approbation, am, though vnworthie, a speaker for others, may be permitted to become an humble suitor for my self to y^r excellent Matie, that y^u would be pleased to cover my errors & defectes wth the vaile of gratious construction ; & to extend to me y^r most humble servant, the first of all others that in publicke needs & craves it, y^r free & gratious pardon.

Page 20.   this oration of the Speakers had this answer by/ the Keeper according to the formalitie of the time. the interim was little, yet awhile hee seemd to studie the recollection of some notes he then had taken: but that trouble was not much, nor needed it at all, wch being done, he thus deliver'd what formerlie was agreed on.

Mr Speaker his Matie hath heard y^u wth approbation, both pleading for y^r self, & for y^r countrie, wherin it far'd wth y^u as formerlie wth Gubertus, for if y^u had pleaded ill, wch you were not wont to doe, yet that could not have preiudic'd the opinion of yr service, wch former merites have indeard; but otherwise, as y^u have, making knowne y^r abilitie by y^r eloquence, it confirmes the reputation wch y^u had in the iudgment of his Matie, from whom I am commanded in part to make y^u answer. yr speech was like that perfect bodie of the world, soe orbicular & round, that ther seem'd noe angle in it, but in such a symetrie compos'd, as humors well digested in the bodie, that ther is noe predominance, but in the equall

Page 21.   temper of them all, they make one pure/ complexion: yet in that rotunditie, as the latter Mathematicians have observd, some stops & pointes ther may be found; that perfit bodie has some veines though shadowed artificiallie by the skinne, by wch we may see the blood & spirit conveyd to the severall partes & members in their spheares, & by those stops & pointes take the commensuration of the whole, wch I shall doe in touching some perticulars. Somewhat of y^r self y^u spake & the last parliament; somewhat of his Maties entrance to his raigne & therin of his beginning wth a Parliament, of his descent & blood, of his succession, of his hopes, of his deliverance out of Spaine ; somewhat y^u spake likewise of religion, & the recommendation of that iewell to the K[ing] by the pietie of his ffather at his dyinge; somewhat of the common Lawe as the principle of this goverment; somewhat for the releiving of our frinds ; & somewhat for the repressing of our enemyes, the restraint of preistes & Jesuites; & lastlie of those vsuall petitions for freedome of/ persons, libertie of speech, access vpon occasion, & benigne interpretation of proceedings ; to wch I will answear breiflie in this order & methode I propound them.

ffirst concerning y^r self, who say little but doe much, having once offred to his Matie the sacrifice of y^r lips, & that not being accepted, then, what is better, the offering of obedience, wch these first fruites doe witness, being the oblation of y^r hart, *fœlix faustumq sit*, as was the issue of that Parliament wch concluded wth K[ing] J[ames] & may be well stil'd happie, making a reconciliation betweene his Matie & his subiectes, & a breach & dissolution of those treaties betwixt his enemies & him. the hope & expectation thervpon is yet auspitious to our labors, & the comfort then diffusd from that garland of the Crowne, the king's prerogative, in the flowers that then descended, the bills of grace, cannot but yet affect vs, espetiallie

Page 22.

if we take it from the true rise and ground, the labors & endeavors of his Matie, then heer afsifting vs, who acted not a/ little in that sceane ; this may assure vs much of his future love to Parliamentes, his entrance & initiation being such : he being then to that Parliament (made soe happie) as the Sowle in the bodie of a man, the life & glorie of it, when he receavd such pleasure in this Councell as makes him still to love it. ffor his entrance into goverment, his blood, his succession, & his hopes, & that deliverance out of Spaine, all speake him the sonne of hope & wonder. for what can give more to the satiffaction of his people then this first act of meeting & conferenc[e] heer wth them ? what can add more to the promise of his hopes, then the virtue & nobilitie of the stocke, wherin he is more eminent then anie prince in chriftendome, having *deum in vtroq parente*, as tis said, on both sides, being extracted from a long descent of kings. how has his succession, in point of restitution to the kingdome, made vp that breach wch sorrow had enforc't vpon the loss of his deer ffather, wch could not have beene done, by any but by him, nor by him if he had beene but the/ sonne onlie of his bodie ! those abilities of his ffathers wch are regnant in his sowle, of wch we have had experience, are a sufficient warrant for our hopes ; & those hopes we have confirmd by his miraculous deliverie out of Spaine, wch prove him aswell the adopted sonne of God, as the naturallie begotten of K[ing] J[ames]

divinitie concurring wth his wisdome, & giving that
wifdom to him wch could not be circumvented by
their pollicie: a *noli me tangere*, I may terme him, one
whom noe humane wit can deale wth. ffor religion,
wherin, to the naturall zeale & pietie of his Matie
ther hath beene added such a spurr, by the charge &
blessing of his ffather, we need not doubt his tender
care therof, that principle being implanted in his hart;
but as we have enioy'd vnder the sun shine of the
gospell a long & rare felicitie, soe we shall still
retayne it vnder his princelie providence & see our
Jerusalem in prosperitie all his life long. touching
the common law, wch worthilie you commended, as
the fittest temper for this goverment, his Matie is
soe indulgent to that rule,/ as he recommends it to
their studies who are professors of it, to follow the
antient maximes, not resting on new cases, wch are the
fancies but of men; but to fetch their knowledg from
the principles wch were grounded first on reason, & had
their derivation from God's lawes, in wch they should
want noe favor from his Matie, who was most affectionat
to the ould, willing of reformation in the new, betweene
wch ther is this differenc, besides their originall & the
time, that the conclusions of the latter are peremptorie
& sever, drawne from slight premises & inducements,
wheras the others alwaies have strong premisses to induce them, and yet such sweet conclusions as fweyd
by love, not force. ffor the Pallatinat, & the restitution of our frendes, Mr Speaker, y^u cannot imagine

how it contentes his Matie to see y^r care therin, by wch the naturall sympathie is exprest betweene the head & bodie. y^u as the bodie, concurring wth his Matie the head, in sence & participation of their miseries, who are cheif members of/ the kingdome; nor can it be wher such affections meet that ye actes of Egipt, of Meros should be copied; far be it henc, for the honor of this nation, that it should now desert hir frindes, having beene formerlie soe helpfull vnto strangers: & for his Matie, I am to tell y^u this, that he desires not to live otherwise then in glorie, & that cannot be w^thout restitution of the Pallatinat, wch as it wilbe the whole indeavor of his ma^tie must likewise have y^r aydes to second, & supplie him. ffor the abandoning of those sonns of Bichri the preistes & Jesuites, wch y^u move for, his Matie both approves your religion & devotion, & acknowledges wth St Augustine, that the poorest man on earth has as great interest in religion as the greatest prince or potentat: but, as princes were made keepers of both tables, soe he desires to be trusted wth this suite, wch in fitt time he will either grant, or better it; wherin, as his ffather said before him, he would be as carefull & sincear, as he praied God to be mercifull to him. Lastly Mr Speaker, for thofe petitions y^u exhibited of/ freedome from arrestes, libertie of speech, access vpon occasion, and favorable construction of y^r actions, wch are the fower corner stones of that noble building of y^r house, his Matie grants them all w^thout anie bound or limitation more then y{superscript r} owne wisdoms & modesties shall impose, not doubting, but if anie shall abuse this libertie w{superscript ch} is granted, y{superscript u} wilbe more readie to punishe & correct him, then his Ma{superscript tie} to require it.

these speeches had divers censures w{superscript th} the hearers; first by comparison & in generall, wherin it was noted that the Lawiers expressions were divine, the divines more historicall & lawlike. then in the B{superscript p} was observd both for composition, & deliverie, [that] studie & affectation, w{superscript ch} the other did decline, who seemd more naturall, not less eloquent. either had thofe *igniculi sententiarum* & *flosculi ingeniorum* for his ornament; by y{superscript e} B{superscript p} they were rendred to all satietie & fulness as bewtie set to sale, wheras the other made them like starrs shining in the night, *admirabili quadam illuminatione sed umbram habens & recessum.* in perticular of the B{superscript ps} ther were two thinges much observd, but w{superscript th} different affection & acceptance; the one/ was, his insinuation to new waies, & the fallacie therin vs'd, to intimat, that all that is done by Parliament is parliamentarie, w{superscript ch} had an ill relishe & resent. the other was that passage in his answear for the priviledges, terming them the corner stones o'th house; w{superscript ch} having that expression in that presence was well lik't, it being thervpon presum'd in the opinion of the hearers, that their future eftimation should have answeard it. but that difcourfe being formall, & noe more, had not such influence on the act. states, as divines, vse glosses on their texts. but for the inftant, fatiffaction was pretended, & both houses thervpon prepar'd them to their business.

Page 28.

The Commons begann wth an Act for observation of the Sabboth, & to prevent the abuses of that daie, wch being read, for the honor of religion & to that end having the first precedence given it ; further to express the devotion of the house expecting all blessings from above ; the next thing that followd it was the desire of a Communion that all the members of that bodie might ioyne & in that worke of pietie, the better to vnite them in themselves, & reconcile them to their head ; & this/ religious motion was forthwth seconded by another for a day of preparation to that worke & a generall humiliation to be made, by a publicke fast i'th kingdome, for wch foure reasons were assign'd. 1. the miseries of the church abroad. 2. the plague & mortalitie at home. 3. the ffleet & preparation then in hand. 4. the expectation of the Parliament ; to implore a blessing vpon thefe ; to deprecat the calamities of the others ; wch reasons were approv'd & the desires resolv'd on. the Communion was appointed for the Sundaie sennight after, & a Committee nam'd to see that all performd it. the privat fast & preparation was to precede it on the Saturdaie. preachers were design'd for both ; and it was ordered for the generall fast o'th kingdome that a petition should be fram'd to move his Matie therin. wch actes of pietie being resolv'd, they defcended to the ordinarie bufinefs of the house, &, as the manner is, in the firft place appointed a Com^{tee} for their priviledges, that being thought most necessarie to precede, by wch their powers & being did subsift. the intention of that Com^{tee} wch is standing & not tranfient, has/ a generall reflection on their rights, & on all actes of preiudice that impeach them, to examine, to discuss them for the ease and information of the house, that ther they may be punisht, or prevented : but the ordinarie agitations wch it has, are for elections & returnes, to rectifie the obliquities therin, wch are in all times manie, in some more, wherof ther wanted not a large proportion even in that. amongst others of that kinde, the Com^{tee} being setled, a petitiòn was exhibited to the house against the returne for yorkshire. the partie complaininge was Sr John Savill, his cheife opposit then returnd, Sr Thomas Wentworth, whofe contestation in the countrie had beene great, as their former emulation in that place, nor wanted they a reputation good in either, nor meritt, if well exercis'd to support it. I mention heer but that perticular of Wentworth, because the whole businefs turnd on him, his colleague in that service being but passive in the worke, & soe involvd wth him, as what was accidentall to the one was necessarilie contingent to the other, for the qualitie & meritt of their cause, the same virtue/ & the same fortune being to both. for the present the petition was refer'd to the Com^{tee} to be first heard & treated of. after this & some others of that kinde, wch had like reference from the house, an vnexpected motion was delivered to decline the whole proceedings of that meeting, & to petition for an adiornment to the K[ing]. the reason pretended was the sickness, wch had a great infection & increase : but most men did suppose that but the color & pretext, & something more wthin it, wch ielosie the sequell did confirme.

Page 31.

it had it's originall from the north, & by some other northerne spirits was seconded, who after practisd all the artifice of delaie to deferr the question of their knightes, & since have beene declar'd soe affected to themselves, & to their owne advancements, that all confideration of iustice & the publicke they postpon'd. this proposition being on foote was soe farr prest and followd, vpon the reasons & argumentes given against it, as the elect of yorkshire came in perticular to oppose the business propounded by the K[ing] & for that vrg'd the accompt that was behinde for the subsidies & fifteenths given in the/ former Parliament, saying it was more necessarie that that accompt were rendred, then to require new aydes ; to wch it was replied, that nothing did lett the accompt, but that satiffaction might be had, & for the new demand, the time, the world, themselves might iudge how farr necessarie it was, & exceeding the termes of that comparison. for the adiornment twas obiected to be contrarie to the order of the houfe, wch in the fast implied a resolution of their fitting, to wch end was desird the publicke praiers o'th church to implore a blessing on their labors, wch if they then declin'd, that act of devotion was in vaine, & the practise and profession were incongruous. the danger of the sickness was confest, & that ballanc't wth the danger of the enemyes, vpon wch David's example was induc'd for a direction in the case, that shewd it better, to fall into the righteous hands of God, then into the wicked hands of men. other reasons were added vnto these, as, it being the first meetinge wth the K[ing], the expectation great vpon it, the reputation of much importance that should follow it, wch wth the former, soe sweyd the sence o'th house, as, though noe names were vs'd to turne/ it, seeking onlie an alteration of the place, not of the time & bufiness; yet the motion was reiected as improper, & by some held ominous & portentous. thefe were the agitations of that daie, & the initiation of the business. the next (after the bill o'th Sabboth read againe, when it receav'd commitment) motion was made for the grand Com^tee of the GREIVANCES, vpon wch ther did arise a new trouble & dispute. but before we proceed to that, I thinke it not vnnecessarie that we a little heer insist vpon that vse & naming of Com^tees, wch being opend heer we shall the better know it els wher, & soe difcerne more eafilie, both in the execution & designe, the scope & intention of those orders. ther are three grand Com^tees consisting of the whole house, onlie the speaker leaving the formalitie of his chaire, wch are permanent & standing, & vsually appointed in the beginning of the Parliamentes, for religion, greivances, & Courts of Justice; these have their severall weeklie daies assign'd them, & take generall cognisance of all matters,/ examine all complaints, send for all persons & recordes; all corruptions & iniustices of Courtes, exactions of their Ministers, oppressions of the people, abuses & enormities in the church are respectivlie the subiectes of their treaties. thefe they difcusse & handle for the knowledg of the facts; & if they finde them faultie, worthie a publicke judgment, thenc they are reported to the house, wch thervpon proceeds to censure & determine them. privat Com^tees, wch are transient, & selected, of some few proportionable to the cause, have in their sphears & compass an equall power & interest. those that are for bills on the second reading are defignd, the first being onlie formall, when seldome, or never they are spoken to, but in pointe of reiection & deniall, & that rarelie, if ther be color for the intention, though ther be imperfections in the draught : but at the second reading all obiections doe come in(.) the perticulars both of the forme & matter, are then argued & debated, & thervpon it passes to Commitment, wher by answear & replie the difcussion may be freer in the counterchange of reason & opinion (wch is not admittable in the house, wher to avoyd conteftation/ & diforder, wch replies & contradictions might induce, & to preserve the gravitie, noe man may speake in one daie, & to one bufiness, above once, though he would change opinion, (wch in Com^tees is allowable) & therfore vpon the second readings of these bills they have such reference & commitment, that ther they may the more punctuallie be considered, & soe come to the exacter reformation & amendment. In generall, all Com^tees are for preparation & dispatch : the iudgment & conclufion is the house's ; to facilitat that Court in the multiplicitie of hir labors, these are the Argus & Briarius ; these Com^tees are the sentinells vpon all affaires & interestes, & these dissolve the difficulties wch their greatness or numbers doe import. According to these customes & reasons of the former, in this Parliament it was mov'd likewise for the Com^tee of the Greivances, as we before observ'd it. divers oppositions it receav'd for divers interestes & respectes, publicke & privat, wherin contraries did meet. Some did dislike it for accident & circumstance, others simplie & absolutlie for it self; that it might have reflection on their errors who were/ conscious of a guilt made these others being Page 36. obnoxious to the publicke. others that thought it not seasonable at that time to begin the question of those greivances, wch could not then be perfitted, for the more certayne punishment of the offenders would have their cause reservd. others were movd in apprehension of the sickness, to decline that service, for the dismission of petitioners. some had in contemplation the new entrance of the K[ing] whose raigne had not afforded opportunitie for oppressing, & should not therfore be dishonord wth an asperfion of complaint. others remembred the ould greivances exhibited to K[ing] J[ames] in his last Parliament, to wch ther had beene noe answear, & advisd onlie to petition then for that. but none of these reasons could prevaile to compose the affection of the house, wch to that Com^{tee} for the greivances added likewife a desire of the other for religion, & therin vrg'd the great danger & necessitie vpon the practise of the Jesuits, the insinuation of the prieftes, the exercise of the masse, in despight, ir not derifion, of the lawes; & the confidence/ & increase of Page 37. papistes thervpon; wch plague & infection of the sowles, was farr more to be feared then all the plagues & infections of the bodie. this, wth the new occasion, stir'd a new sence i'th house & raisd the argumentes wch did follow it to a more heigth & quickness, for allay wherof this Catho-

K

licon, being prepar'd by that great artist Sr Ben. Ruddiard, was readilie presented to the occaſion, & in this forme applied.

Mr. Speaker to say this is the first Parliament of the K[ing] is noe great matter: but that the first Parliament of the K[ing] should have a temperat proceeding & propitious success is a matter of extraordinarie consideration & consequenc; for it is commonlie seene that the same influenc wch governs in the beginning of an action infuseth it self throughout, & continues to the end, as in this perticular of Parliamentes we have had too deer experience. certainlie the disagreement betwixt the K[ing] who is wth God, & his people, begun & continued by mutuall distasts in Parliament, have beene the cause almost of all that/ we can call amiss in this State. it was the K[ing] wch now is, who first gave the happie turne in the last, wherin I may trulie say, ther descended more grace from the Crowne to the subiect then in any Parliament some hundreds of years before; & I may rehears, though not obiect, that wee also did our duties. if his Matie when he was prince, & had but a mediating intereſt did vs so manie good offices, soe manie gratious favors, what may we expect now that he is K[ing] & hath absolut power in his owne hands? we may well trust him whom we have soe well tried, especiallie seeing he gives vs dailie new argumentes of his goodneſs & wisdome. how publicklie & frequentlie he avowes and iustifies, his owne, the true religion, wth discountenance to the fals? how effectuallie this devotion of his workes vpon his life, insomuch as I may stricktlie say ther can hardlie be found a privat man of his years soe free from all ill? wch as it is more rare & difficult in the/ person of a K[ing] soe is it more exemplar & extensive in the operation, & noe doubt, being a blessing in it self, will call downe more blessings from heaven vpon this kingdom for his sake. ffor his wisdome, we see that in his perticular actions he is naturallie regular & orderlie, wch however some retir'd abstruse spirites may accompt but a formalitie; yet wise men know how much it conduceth to wealth, to greatness, to goverment; order being indeed the verie soule of outward things. befides his breeding hath given him an advantage above all the kings in christendome; for he hath beene abroad, & hath treated wth a wise & subtile nation in a business soe great, as himself was the subiect of it, wch hath not onlie open'd & enlarg'd but quicken'd & sharpned his naturall abilities, & made him vnderstand his owne kingdome the better; for to know a man's owne countrie alone is but a solitarie kind of knowledg in respect/ of knowing it by comparison wth others. but that wch is of most vse & application to vs is that he hath beene bred in Parliamentes, wch hath made him not onlie to know but to favor the waies of his owne subiectes, wherof it becomes vs alwaies to have a gratefull remembrance. vpon these foundations

Page 39.

Page 40.

Mr. Speaker, I will humblie move this honorable house in that wherin I hope we are all come hither prepar'd & mov'd in our selves, that is to carrie our selves in this first session wth sweetness, wth dutie, wth confidence in & towardes his Matie, for wch noe doubt, we shall respectivlie receave such grace, such favor, such satiffaction as the dangerousness of the time & therfor the shortness of it can possiblie allowe. towards the happie effecting wherof I doe further move, that we may fall vpon such things onlie, as are necessarie, cleer & of dispatch; & that those businesses wch have in them either perplexitie, difficultie, or asperitie, if the house be not pleas'd/ altogether to omitt them, yet they may be onlie touch't by way of claime or greivance & soe remitted to the next session, when we shall have fitter opportunitie & better leasure to debate them. Last of all to take off the least scruple of preiudice wch misinterpretation may cast vpon me, I doe heer solemnlie protest, that, as heertofore I did never speake with K[ing], prince or favorit, of Parliament business, soe wth our present K[ing], I never had the honor to speake fourtie words of any purpose what soever; insomuch as what I have said, I have spoken it out of the sinceritie of myne owne hart, wthout anie other end but the good of the Commonwealth, wherof this assemblie is the abridgment.

this oration in much gravitie delivered, wth the length & expectation that it carried, had somuch of the effect, as it reduc'd to temper the affection that was stir'd. all mens intentions still went wth it to observe the conclusions it would make. a great reputation was implied both in the learninge & wisdome of the man; & as he was/ in vse & estimation wth some great ones, more was expected from him then from others, wch made the satiffaction to seeme less, & those that were more criticall to adiudge his composition more studied then exact. all men difcernd in him noe want of affection to be eloquent: but his expression was thought languid as the conclusion was enapt; generalls being fitter for discourse then in counfell or debate. yet soe farr this prevaild, or els the time by that, as the resolution was defer'd to a further confideration & dispute, & soe the present heat declin'd. wch is obfervable in that house, as their whole storie gives it, that wher ever that mention does breake of the fears or dangers in religion, & the increase of poperie, their affections are much stir'd, & what ever is obnoxious in the State, it then is reckoned as an incident to that: for soe it followd vpon the agitation of that motion, first the danger of religion was obferv'd in some generall notes of preiudice; then by induction it was provd in the enumeration of perticulars; to that was vrg'd the infelicities of the kingdome since that difease came in. this/ had an aggravation by a syneresis & comparifon wth the daies of Q[ueen] El[izabeth]. to that was added the new greivances & oppressions, whollie infer'd & raisd since the connivence wth the papistes: the monopolies that had beene, the ímpositions that then were, all were reduc'd to this; wch I mention but to shew the apprehension in that pointe, & the affection of that house in matter of religion.

the next daie was begunne wth a conference of both houses vpon the petition for the fast. at the conference the Commons did present a draught of the petition & their reasons, wth a motion to the Lords for their concurrenc in the worke, who by that reverend ffather of the church, the Archbishop of Canterburie, returnd this answear & replie. that they approved both their intention & their reasons, & were therein readie to assist them; but wth all, out of a text in Joel, gave them such a caution & advise against privat vndertakings of that kinde, as vpon their returne vnto their house, the former daie was altered & some time given for expectation in that pointe. after/ this the dispute of religion was resum'd, wherin some introduction being made, it was thus followd for preparation & advise.

⁎ religion is the touchstone of all actions, the triall by wch they are knowne, vpon wch all pollicie, all wisdome, all excellenc must be grounded, & what rests not on this center can have noe perfection or assurance: for what the power of man is wth out God, or what wth out religion, may be expected from his favor, his owne wordes & stories doe sufficientlie declare. religion onlie it is that fortifies all pollicie, that crownes all wisdome, that is the grace of excellenc; the glorie of all power, the strength of all goverment is religion; for though pollicie might secure a kingdome against forraigners (& soe I praise God this kingdom may alwaies stand secure) & wis-

dome provide all necessaries for the rule & goverment at home; yet, if religion season not the affections of the people, the danger is asmuch in our owne Achitopheles as of Moab & all the armies of/ Philistims. religion it is that keeps the subiect in obedience, as being taught by God to honor his vicegerentes. a *religando* it is cal'd, as the common obligation amongst men, the tye of all frindship & societie, the band of all office & relation, writing everie dutie in the conscience, wch is the stricktest of all lawes. both the excellence & necessitie heerof the heathens knew, that knew not true religion, & therfore in their polliticks they had it alwaies for a maxime : a shame it were for vs to be therin less intelligent then they, & if we trulie know it we cannot but be affectionat in this case.

Page 45.

two things are considerable therin, the puritie, the vnitie therof; the first respecting onlie God, theother both God & man; for wher ther is division in religion as it does wrong divinitie it makes distractions amongſt men, & soe dissolves all ties & obligations, civill & naturall, the observation of heaven being more powerfull then either pollicie or blood. ffor the puritie of religion in this place I need not speake, seeing how bewtifull the/ memories of our ffathers are therin made by their indeavors. ffor the vnitie I wishe posteritie might say we had preserved for them that wch was left to vs; but a difease once enterd, though it be past prevention, must have cure, & as the danger or infec-

Page 46.

tion becomes greater, the greater care & diligence must oppose it.

what divifions, what factions, naie what fractions in religion this kingdome does now suffer, I need not recapitulat. what diverfions, what transactions, what alienations have beene made noe man can be ignorant. how manie members, in that pointe, have been dissected from this bodie, I meane the bodie of the land, wch representativlie we are, soe as the bodie it self, though healthie, cannot but seeme lame? how have those members studied to be incorporat wth others? how have they threatend vs, their owne, not onlie by presumption but in greatness, & given vs far more then they have taken? blessed be that hand that has deliverd vs, blessed this daie that gives vs hope, wherin the danger & infection may be stai'd; for wth out present remedie/ the disease will scarce be curable.

to effect this the cause must first be sought from whenc this sickness springs, & that wilbe best found in the survey of the lawes, for certainlie it lies in the lawe, or execution; either ther is some defect or imperfection in the lawes, or their life, the execution is remitted: for if the lawes be perfect, how can division enter but by a breach of them? if the execution be obferv'd how can the lawes be broken? therfore in this does rest the cause, & heer must be the remedie. to that end now my motion shall encline for a review o'th lawes & a speciall confideration in that pointe, that if ye divifion have gott in by imperfection of the lawes they may be amended ; if by defect that may be supplied ; if, as I most doe fear it, through neglect, & want of execution, the power may be enforc't wth some great mulct & penaltie on the miniſters, who for that wilbe more vigilant & we therby secure.

this speach gave occaſion for à generall conſideration/ of the lawes, wherin it was confest ther was a sufficiencie & fulness, but the want of execution did impaire it, & both detract from the power & reputation of the lawes. in this divers perticulars were instanc't, some to prevent, some to corrupt the lawes. in some ther was observ'd to be *fraus legis*, a cousenage of the lawe, & that former waies effected. first, by dependanc on great men, wch were a terror to informers, & wthout them noe delinquentes could be found. secondlie, by changing names & appellations, practisd both by papistes preistes & Jesuites, who by the often shift of places, soe did avoid indictmentes. thirdlie by procuring information against themselves, wch th⸱y could press or stop & soe preventing others in the like manner, as a *supersedeas* for the peace. fowerthlie, by certioraries removing the indictmentes from the Countries, soe as noe prosecutor should be found, & soe noe more proceeding. & in others ther was noted to be *fraus contra legem*, an abuse & cousenage of the K[ing] for what the lawe allowd him. & of this likewise ther were fower waies defcribd. first by removing of their goods into priviledg'd & free/ places, soe as noe forfeiture could be served. then by begging of such forfeitures by those about the K[ing], who intended not the punishment, but favor of the papistes.

Page 48.

Page 49.

thirdlie by letters procur'd in their behalf for stop & prohibition of proceedings. & lastlie by the pardons, wch too frequentlie were granted, not onlie to recusants but to Jesuites. all wch did hinder the execution of the lawes & renderd them fruitless. in that pointe, & were designd for causes of that difease & sickness. examples were cited of all thefe to warrant their reasons & opinions, wherof it was thought necessarie ther should be a true information to the K[ing], & an address & petition to reforme them. for a preparation to that worke the clarke was appointed to bring in all the petitions of that kinde, wch formerlie had beene made, at the next sitting, vnto wch the further consideration was refer'd. the next daie, some Com^{tees} of both houses having attended on the [King] reported his answear to the petition for the fast, wch was, that as he lik't their method in beginning wth devotion, soe he did hope ther proceedings would be answearable,

Page 50.   that he approved of the desire/ & after consultation wth the Bishops, would give it execution. ffrom this againe, some few bills being read & that of the Saboth, vpon the third reading, past for lawe, the Commons resum'd againe the consideration of religion, & in that part began wher they had left it last. the former petitions were then read, wch had beene exhibited in 18 & 21 Ja[mes] wth the protestation of the prince made then vpon the sence of his deliverance out of Spaine. from w^{ch} & the disputes that had beene past ther was a Com^{tee} then appointed to frame a new petition to the K[ing]. the Lords about this time having resolvd vpon their fast by message did intimat their time & place to the Commons, who thervpon determin'd

for themselves likewife to have the same daie appointed, &
to strengthen in this service their correspondence by the
place, one church being not capable of both houses, as the
Lords did take the Abby, they chose the parishe church at
westminster, in wch their commu̱nions were before, & now
their firſt of faſtes. thefe pointes of religion thus dispos'd,
wch by/ a former order of the house were to have cleer Page 51.
precedence before all things, the proposition was admitted
for supplie. some art ther was to extenuat the proportion,
& therfor it was begun by a gentleman of the Countrie,
who, vnexpected to the Courtiers, falling on that subiect
& pitching on a perticular of one subsidie & fifteenth, all
their rhetoricke & labor could hardlie thence remove it,
but the inclination of the house still resorted to that
principle. againe heer Sr Ben. Rudyard was imploied,
who but at such times, & in such services, did speake,
never but premeditated, wch had more shew of memorie
then affection, & made his words less powerfull then obfervd. he did deduce his reason for the enlargment of
the ayd from the occafions & necessities of the State.
these he enforc't by the domesticke charge of the K[ing],
the funerall of his ffather, the entertaynement of Ambaſ-
sadors, the forraigne expences & ingagmentes to Denmarke,
Manffeilt, & the States, befides/ his owne preparations then Page 52.
for warr; all wch he said requird a vast supplie of treasure
& that must have it's magazine on the people. noe particular summe he inſtanc't, wch made his reasons less succesfull, & soe, in that respect his labor was in vaine. yet
divers others follow'd him, & in divers waies & motions.

some would have an addition of fifteenths, others of subsidies, & ther were that preſt for both : but in little they prevaild. the pitch being sett at first was not soe easilie exceeded; yet the *quindecim* thought greivous to the poore, changd the proposition in that part. wch was concluded in the whole for two subſidies alone. to endear both the proportion & the gift, divers circumstances were observd of force & aggravation. first the time, it being then but the beginning of a Parliament, wheras supplie was antientlie a worke of the conclusion. then that the grant it self intended was of that value, as not fower Kings of England ever had the like. then that the condition of the people, though the manie violation[s]/ of their rights, in the generall liberties of the kingdom, the perticular priviledges of that house, their burdens, their oppressions, which noe times els could parallell, spoke them less able; & that complaint postposd, shew'd them more affectionat. then that ther was noe ingagment to induce it, as manie had suppos'd vpon the declaration of the last parliament of K[ing] J[ames], that promise being made for supportation of a warr, & yet ther being noe knowledg of an enemye. againe the former grant was spoken of, for wch ther had beene noe reckoninge ; & theron, by way of question twas digrest, to conſider what accompt was answearable for the manie thousand men, that had perisht & beene lost, in the Pallatinat, & wth Manffeilt; the millions of treasure that was spent, w^thout success, in profit or honor to the kingdome, wch was noted not to be England's ffate, when God & it were frindes; & for that the glories of Q [ueen]

El[izabeth] were inftanc't, who wth less supplies and aydes, encreasd hir self at home, wasted hir enemies abroad,/ consum'd Spaine, raifd the Low Countries, reviv'd ffrance. vpon all w[ch] it was desir'd, that ther might be a petition to the K[ing], to move him to consideration of those things, & to reforme the goverment, then at his entrance & beginning by the like counfell & advise ; w[ch] petition & remonstrance would tell him from those reafons, how affectionat was that grant. & it was added by him that foe deduc'd it, that he was soe farr from augmentation, as he would have noe man heard to move it. this being rendred by Sr Robert Philips wth a great life & eloquence movd much in the apprehension of the house, both for the setling of that question, & this reflection on the times. the present povertie was felt in the generall necessities of the Countrie. the cause of that was knowne to be the greivances and oppressions. the loss of men, loss of honor, loss of monie, the late infortunities of K[ing] J[ames] were too obvious & vndoubted, as the contrarie felicities of Q[ueen] El[izabeth] soe as all men of themselves sawe the present want of Councell, & some resolvd, in time, more specially to complaine it. ther was in this gentleman/ a naturall grace of oratorie, a moving & Nestorean waie of rhetoricke, a choise store he had & elegance of wordes, readiness & dexteritie in fancie & conception ; a voice & pronunciation of much sweetness. the whole expression, *profluens & canora*; but, as some iudgd of Cicero, by some thought in him to be *tumens & exultans*. a redundancie & exuberance he had, & an

Page 54.

Page 55.

affected cadence & deliverie. but vpon all occaſions, at all times, *ex re nata*, he was rendred, wch made his argumentes, as more genuine & perticular, soe more acceptable, & perſwaſive: for in that place alwaies premeditation is an error, all speech of composition & exactness, being suppoſed, *ex ore non a pectore*, & those children of the mouth onlie are not somuch affecting as the true issues of the hart. this spell was a charme vpon the Courtiers to suppress their further craving: yet something was added by the rest for the improvement of this gift, that the recuſantes should pay double, wch after some small letts was likewise accorded & concluded on, wherof the acceptation & success shall be noted in their orders./ that great worke being done, an accompt was represented from the Archbishop of Canterburie of his proceedings wth Mountague vpon the reference of that house in the last parliament of K[ing] J[ames] wch was, that, having convented him before him, and tould him of the troubles he had caus'd, & what disturbance was growen in the church & in the Parliament by his booke; he gave him this advice, Be occaſion of noe scandall; goe home, reveiwe y^r booke, it may be some things have slip't y^u, wch vpon second cogitations y^u will reforme. if anie thing be said toomuch, take it away; if anie thing too little add vnto it; if anie thing be obſcure explaine it but doe not wedd y^rself to y^r owne opinion; & remember we must give accompt of our ministerie to Christ: wth wch admonition being dismiſt, it was said, he heard noe more of him for a long time after, till, one daie going to attend vpon the K[ing] he came suddanlie vpon

Page 56.

him, & presented him, *in cursu*, as it were, his second booke; for wch being shortlie question'd, as the place & time permitted, of that bouldness & neglect, he made a slight answear & departed. this carriage/ and report were Page 57. diverslie interpreted & receavd. some did wonder at the insolence of Mountague, that˜ he dar'd soe affront the dignitie of that ffather; for it was held noe less, instead of a retraction for the former, to present a second booke in confirmation of the other for wch he had beene question'd, & to publishe it w^th[out] the knowledg of the Archbishop. others did thinke it strange, the lenitie of the Archbishop, that he would pass vnpunished such an indignitie to his place, his person likewise being iniur'd in the fact. but those that look't more narrowlie conceav'd one reason for both these, & both that bouldness in the one, & remisness of the other by command. againe the admonition given, though grave, was neither represive, nor directing, being but made in generalls, & that by way of supposition & hypothesis, wch hardlie answear'd the expectation that was had. but this also was imagined the same power of influence had wrought. K[ing] J[ames] was knowne then secretlie to support him. the Archbishop did confess that he was twice w^th/ the K[ing] sent for in that business, Page 58. wch being opend, few men did after doubt by whom that sceane was made. yet it seemd strange to some that K[ing] J[ames] should soe affect him. his doctrines being oppos'd to the decisions made at Dort, & that Synod being sqe honor'd by the K[ing], of wch he assum'd the patronage, & somuch gloried in it. this man being opposit, *ex diametro*, to that, & his bookes likewise casting divers aspersions on the K[ing] as will hearafter be obfervd, manie did wonder how these things could agree, w^{ch}, as a secret rested vpon a higher principle. but this report being made, the house againe resumd the cognisance of that matter to themselves, & referd the examinations of the bookes to the Com^{tee} for religion. this past the first daie of Julie, the fourth the king's Sollicitor did exhibit an answear to the greivances formerlie complain'd of to K[ing] J[ames] wch because they doe express much of reason of that time, & the inclination of the State, we will perticularlie heer insert them, as we have done the greivances elswher, noting onlie but the heades that were complain'd of for the better illustration of their answears./

1. against the patent for the plantation of new England.

ans. it shalbe free for all the Kings subiectes to performe their fishing voyages, vpon that coast, yeilding a reasonable recompence to the patentees for their wood and timber, & if anie thing in the patent be against lawe it shalbe amended.

2. against the incorporation of gouldwire-drawers.

ans. the patent is in the clarke of the Parliament his hands, & is not vs'd; & his Matie is well pleas'd that it be recal'd by course of lawe, if they will not voluntarilie surrender it.

3. agst the patent of concealments granted to Sr John Townshend.

ans. the patent is delivered to the clark of the Parliament, & it is not vsed ; & if it be thought fit to be revok't by bill, his Matie will pass it.

4. ag^st licences cal'd breifes.

ans. his Matie hath commanded none to be granted/ but vpon certificat in open Sessions, & that such certificats shall not be made, but vpon iust cause, & that the same be alwaies one. Page 60.

5. ag^st the patent of apothecaries.

ans. if anie thing in these letters patentes be amiss in the manner & forme, his ma^tie leaves it to the Parliament to be reformd by bill: but because it concernes the life & health of his subiectes, he doth not think it fit, it should be left w^thout goverment in the meane time.

6. ag^st Sr John Mildrams patent of the light of winter towness.

ans. this light is vsefull & necessarie, but if the tax be too great, he wisheth it may be moderated, wch he refers to the advice of both the Houses.

7. ag^st Sr Symon Harvie.

ans. the particular abuses have been examined & the compositions wch were the ground of the misdeameanoure are set at large.

8. ag^st grantes of the Cuſtodie of Jailes to other/ then Sheriffes. Page 61.

ans. the sheriffes shall according to lawe have the custodie of Jailes in those places wch are in the king's hands, & all grantes to the contrarie are left to the lawe.

9. ag^st the patent of Surveyorship of new-castell-coales.

ans. this patent hath had noe continuance from his Matie, & the validitie of it is left at the lawe

10. ag^st ye multitude of popish & seditious bookes.

ans. a proclamation was latelie made to reforme the abuses in this kinde, which shalbe renew'd.

11. agst the proclamation for buildings.

ans. ther hath much good come by the reformation of buildings, & such pointes as were formerlie found inconvenient are now qualified & altered, and his Matie is resolved to goe forward wth the work.

12. agst D^r. Anian./

ans. when they of the colledg doe complaine to his Matie, his Matie will take care of them.

13. concerning the instructions of the Courtes of wardes.

ans, his Matie will recall the last inftructions & will establish new according to the[ir] desire.

14. agst the marchant adventurers, (wch part of the petition consisting of divers articles, they had these severall answears).

 ans. 1. the trade of cloth is quickned & noe complaint since the last year.

 2. the maine causes of the decay are remov'd. dyed & drest clothes may be vented by anie other to all places, except those limitted to the marchant adventurers; new manufactures by anie other to anie place. & if white clothes be not bought by the adventurers anie other shall have leave to buy them.

 3. the imposition laid by the Marchant adventurers is abated & limitted to a shorter time, & afterwards to be laid by.

 4. his ma^{tie} will write to his Ambassadors wth the Archdutchess & States concerning the burdens laid vpon cloth in those partes.

NEGOTIUM POSTERORUM. 83

5. his Matie hath not time to examine the/ preter- Page 63.
mitted Customes, but leaves it to the next
Session.
6. the ffees of the custome house shalbe regulated
& tables appointed.
15. concerninge the complaint of the Levant Marchantes.
ans. the imposition is not new, nor more then was in
Q[ueen] El[isabeths] time. & the Venetians offer
to bear it, soe as they may bring in their commodities,
wch they will doe in English bottoms, wch takes away
the pretence of overcharge.
16. ag^st the patent of Pennie & Gennie.
ans. this patent is delivered into the handes of the clarke
of the Parliament, & is left to the lawes.
17. ag^st the abuse of alnage.
ans. the abuses of the deputie alnagers are directed to be reformed by speciall limitations.
18 concerning perpetuana's & searges.
ans. the rates vpon the searges & perpetuana's have beene
complaind of by the westerne marchantes & are
moderated to their content.
19. ag^st the abuses of prisage./
ans. prisage shall not be taken but according to the rule of Page 64.
iustice.[1]
20. concerning cloth workers.
ans. his Matie leaves it to the Parliament to consider what
is to be done therin.
21. concerning tobacco.
ans. his Matie hath prohibited all foraigne tobacco & none is to
be imported but of the growth of his owne dominions.

22. concerning the East Land Marchantes.
ans. the marchantes doe give way that anie other may bring in necessaries for shipping & timber.
23. concerning the impositions vpon currance.
ans. the Venetians are contented to bear this charge soe they may have the importation, & they will bring none but in English bottoms.

 divers exceptions were made at manie of these answears, & little satisfaction vpon all ; but the occasion & complaint being of former time, this was accepted for the present, though the hope & expectation wch was had, from thence foorth did decline.

 The sickness was then risen to a great infection & mortalitie, noe part of the citie did stand free./
 divers fell dead downe in the streetes. all companies & places were suspected, wch made all men willing to remove, & those of the Parliament more readie to shorten & expedit their business. to that end the petition for religion was then speeded, & imparted in a conference to the Lords, who therin concurring as the mutuall act of both, it was in this forme presented to the K[ing].

 Most gratious Souvraigne

  It being infalliblie true that nothing can more establish y^r throne & assure the peace & prosperitie of y^r people then the vnitie & sinceritie of religion ; we y^r Maties most humble & loiall subiectes the Lords spirituall & temporall, & Commons in this present Parliament assembled, obferving that of late ther is an apparant mischievous increase of Papistes in y^r dominions, hould our selves bound in concience & dutie to represent the same to y^r Sacred Matie, togeather wth the dangerous consequences, & what we conceave to be the principall causes therof, & what may be the remedies./

the dangers appeer in theise perticulars.   Page 66.

1. their desperat ends, being the subversion both of the Church & State; & the restlessness of their spirites to attaine those endes; the doctrine of their teachers & leaders perfuading them that therein they shall doe God good service.
2. their evident & strick't dependancie vpon such forraigne princes as noe waie affect the good of y^r Matie & this State.
3. the opening a way of popularitie to the ambition of anie wch shall adventure to make him self head of soe great a partie.

the principall causes of the increase of papistes are these.

1. the want of due execution of the lawes against Jesuites, seminarie preistes, & popish recusantes, occasioned partlie by connivence of the State, partlie by some defectes in the lawes themselves, & partlie by the manifould abuses of officers.
2. the interposing of fforraigne princes by their Ambassadors & agentes in favor of them.
3. their great concurse to the Citie, & their/ frequent con- Page 67. venticles & conference ther.
4. their open & vsuall resort to the houses & chappells of fforraigne Ambassadors.
5. the education of their children in Seminaries & houses

of their religion in fforraigne partes, wch of late haue been greatlie multiplied & inlarged for entertayning of the English.
6. that in some places of this yr Realme your people are not sufficientlie instructed in the knowledg of true religion.
7. the licentious printing & dispersing of popish & seditious bookes.
8. the imploiment of men ill affected in religion in places of goverment, who doe, shall, or may countenance the popish partie.

The remedies against this contagious & dangerous disease we conceave to be theise ensuing.

1. that the youth of this kingdom be carefullj educated by able & religious schoolmaifters, & they be enioyned dilligentlie to cathechise & inftruct their schollers in the groundes & principles of religion. & wheras by manie complaintes from divers partes of this kingdom it doth plainlie appeer that sundrie popish/ schoolmafters dissembling their religion, have craftilie crept in, & obtayned the places of teaching in divers countries, & therby infected & perverted their schollers, & soe fitted them to be transported to the popish seminaries beyond te Seas. that therfore ther be great care in the choice & admitting of Schoolmafters, & that the Ordinaries make diligent enquirie of their demeanors, & proceed to the removing of such as shalbe faultie or iustlie suspected.
2. that the Antient discipline of the two Vniversities be

restored, being the ffamous nurceries of litterature & virtue.

3. that speciall care be taken to enlarge the preaching of the word of God through all the partes of y^r Maties dominions as being the most powerfull means for the planting of true religion, & rooting out of the contrarie. to wch end, amongst other things, may it please y^r Matie to advise the Bishops by ffatherlie intreatment & tender vsage, to reduce to the peaceable & orderlie service of the church such able ministers as have/ beene formerlie silenced, that ther may be a profitable vse of their ministrie in these needfull & dangerous times. & that non-residencie, pluralities, & commenda's may be moderated : wher we cannot forbear most humblie to thanke y^r Matie for diminishing the number of y^r owne chaplaines, nothing doubting of y^r like princelie care for the well bestowing of yr benefices, both to the comfort of y^r people & to the encouragement of the Vniversities, being full of grave and able ministers vnfurnished of livings.

4. that ther may be straight provision made against the transportation of Englishe children to the Seminaries beyond the Seas, & for recalling of them, who are ther alreadie placed, & for punishing of such your subiectes as are mayntainers of those Seminaries or of schollers ther, considering that besides the seducing of y^r people, great summs of monie are yeerlie expended vpon them to the impoverishing of this kingdome./

5. that noe popish recusant be permitted to come wthin

the Court vnless y^r ma^tie be pleased to call him vpon speciall occasion, agreeable to the statute 3° Ja. cap 5. & wheras y^r ma^tie for preventing of manie apparant mischeifes both to y^r Matie & this State, have in y^r princelie wisdome taken order, that none of y^r naturall subiectes not professing the said true religion by lawe eftablished, be admitted to the service of y^r most roiall consort the Q[ueen], we give y^r Matie most humble thanks, & desire that y^r order therin may be constantlie observd.

6. that all the lawes now standing in force against Jesuits, Seminarie preistes, and others, having taken orders by authoritie derived from the Sea of Rome, be put in due execution. & to the intent they may not pretend to be surpris'd, that a speedie & certaine daie be prefix't by y^r Maties proclamation for their departure out of this realme, & all other your dominions, & not/ to returne vpon the sevearest penalties of the lawes now in force against them. & that y^r Maties subiectes may be therby also admonished not to receave entertaine comfort or conceale anie of them vpon the penalties wch may be lawfullie inflicted. & that all such preistes, Jesuites & popish recufantes convicted wch are or shalbe imprisoned for recusancie, or anie other cause, may be strictlie restrained, that none may have conference wth them, therby to avoyd the contagion of their corrupt religion. & that none that shal be iustly suspected of poperie be suffered to be keeper of anie of y^r Maties prisons.

7 . That y^r Matie be pleased to take such order as to y^r princelie wisdome shall seeme expedient, that no naturall borne subiect or stranger Bishop, or anie other by authoritie derived from the Sea of Rome, conferr anie ecclesiasticke orders, or exercise anie ecclesiasticall function what soever towardes or vpon any of y^r Maties naturall subiectes wthin anie [of] your dominions./

8. that y^r Mat^{ies} learned councell may receave order & commandment to consider of all former grantes of recusantes landes, that such may be avoyded as are made to they[se] recusantes vse or trust, or out of wch they[se] recusants receave benefit, wch are either void or voidable by lawe.   *Page 72.*

9. that y^r ma^{tie} be likewise pleased straightly to command all iudges & ministers of iustice, both ecclesiasticall & temporall, to see the lawes of this realme against popishe recusantes, to be dulie executed, & namelie, that the censure of excommunication be declared & certified against them. & that they be not obsolved but vpon publicke satiffaction by yeelding to conformitie.

10. that y^r ma^{tie} be pleased to remove from all places of authoritie & goverment all such persons as are either popish recusantes or, according to direction of former Actes of State, iustlie to be suspected.

11. that present order be taken for difarming of all such popish recusantes legallie convicted/or iustlie suspected, according to the lawes in that behalf, & the orders   *Page 73.*

taken by his late Maties privie councell vpon reason of state.

12. that y^r ma^tie be also pleased in regard of the great resort of recusantes to & about London, to command that forthw^th vpon paine of y^r indignation & severe execution of the lawes, they retire themselves to their severall countries, ther to remayne confined w^thin five miles of their dwelling places.

13. & wheras yr Matie hath commanded & taken order that none of y^r naturall subiectes should repair to the hearing of Mass, or other superstitious service, at the chappell, or house of forraigne Ambassadors, or anie other place whatsoever, we give y^r ma^tie most humble thankes; & desire that y^r commandment & order therin may constantlie be observed; & that the offenders therin be punished according to the lawe.

14. that all such insolencies as anie popishly affected have latelie committed, or shall/ heerafter committ, to the dishonor of our religion, or to the wronge of the true professors therof, be exemplarilie punished.

15. that the statute of primo El[isabeth] for the paying of twelve pence everie sunday by such as shalbe absent from divine service in the church w^thout lawfull excuse, may be put in due execution. the rather for that the penaltie is given to the poore by the lawe, and therfore not to be dispensed w^th.

16. Lastlie that y^r Matie be pleased to extend y^r princelie care also over the Kingdome of Ireland, that the like

courses may be ther taken for restoring & establishing of true religion.

And thus moft gratious Soveraigne according to our dutie & zeale to God & religion, to y^r ma^{tie} & y^r saftie, to the church & commonwealth, & their peace & prosperity, we have made a plaine & faithfull diclaration of the present estate; the causes, & remedies of this increasing disease of poperie/ humblie offering the same to y^r Maties princlj care and wisdome. the answear of y^r Maties ffather our late Soveraigne of famous memorie vpon the like petition, did give vs comfort & expectation of a reformation in these things; but y^r Maties manie gratious promises, wch wth much ioye & thankfulnefs we doe remember, doe give vs confident assurance of the continuall performance thereof. In wch comfort and confidence reposing our selves, we most humblie pray for y^r Maties long continuance in all princelie felicitie.

Page 75.

this petition was presented by a Com^{tee} of both houses consisting of the number of   of the lords &   of the Commons, who in all such speciall meetings & Com^{tees} alwaies observe that differenc, that what euer the number be of Lords their proportion is still double it, wch is a fundamentall order of their house, not wth out wisdome in the institution soe appointed, not wth out profit practised on all occafions, &, as it was at other times, soe followd now in this. the petition being delivered had noe answear for the present, but a benigne/ gratious acceptation, the rest, as it was requisit for the state & ma^{tie} of the

Page 76.

prince, & for the weight and importance of the cause, that some time of consideration should be given it; being referd to hope & expectation, all men were therin satiffied that the worke was soe accomplisht, & for success some men presum'd the best.

the next thing wch remayn'd was the bill for the two subfidies that were given, wch likewise being past the house of Commons, & that intimated to the K[ing], it produc'd a message from his ma^tie, wch shortlie after followd it, that gave a generall hope & confidence of a speedie conclusion & recess.

the message was delivered by the Lo. Keeper, the K[ing] being then retir'd to Hampton Court from the danger of the infection; & it came as addrest to both houses, that his ma^tie receav'd great satiffaction & contentment in their guift, both for the forme & matter, it comming as an ernest of their loves. that he tooke into confideration their safties, yea more then his owne in respect of the danger of the sickness still increasing; & that, when he should hear the Commons were readie, though he would not hasten them in anie thing, he would not defer one minute for anie reason to putt an end to/ that sitting by his presence or otherwise. this message & the time wrought soe effectuallie wth all men as what they desird, [that] they easilie did beleeve, & thervpon dispos'd themselves presentlie to retire.

their grant they sawe accepted, & all thinges left to the difcretion of the house. the business then depending was not much, new they presumd would not be receavd; those few questions that remaynd were of noe great importance & most of them but formall, soe as they now conceavd noe necessitie of their presence, & that their non-attendance was dispensable. in this confidence the greatest part went off, hardlie were the Commons a fourth part of their number, & those that staid, resolv'd, wth all the hast they could, to followe those were gone. to that end they tooke a survey of their business. in the first ranck they plac'd the bill of tonnage & poundage, wch then remaynd imperfect, & to this they gave the first confideration for dispatch, & soe a second reading. it was drawne in the vsuall forme, as formerlie it had beene in the daies of K[ing] J[ames] for the like terme of life, & in such latitude as to him ; at wch some exceptions were then made, & motions for change & alteration, vpon w^{ch}/ it was referd for the better difcussion & debate to the grand Com^{tee} of the house, into w^{ch}, the Speaker leaving his chaire, they presentlie resolvd themselves. some did obiect, in that, the exactions of the officers, & the inequalitie of the customes then requird, & vrg'd theron a necessitie for the marchantes to have a new booke of rates, to settle & compose it, wch could not be prepar'd in soe short a time & sitting. others alledgd the pretermitted cuftomes, grounded vpon the misconstruction of that lawe, wch ought to be examind likewise, & the lawes that then remayn'd were thought to be incapable of that worke. therfore on these reafons they inferd a desire for a limitation in the act, & that it might but continue for one year, against wch time, these difficulties being refolvd, they might againe renew it wth a larger extenfion

Page 78.

& continuance. others to this added the question of impositions in the generall & cravd a speciall care not to have that excluded. the elder times were mention'd to note the former grantes, wherin though ther were collected a great varietie & difference, yet all were wthin the limitation of some years: sometimes for one, sometimes for two,/ but seldome above three, & that in ye best raignes & govermentes & to the wiseft princes; never for life till towardes the end of H[enry] 6. in whose beginninges also it had had other limitations & restraintes, & for the time a less extent & latitude. vpon wch likewise it was concluded, for a present alteration in that pointe. the King's Councell opposd this wth much sollicitation & indeavor, & vrg'd the distast it might occasion having somanie descentes held constant in that forme; all the raigne of K[ing] J[ames], all the raigne of Q[ueen] El[isabeth] & soe to Q[ueen] M[ary] E[dward] 6. H[enry] 8. H[enry] 7, & beginning in that raigne, not the most deserving of all others, of H[enry] 6. the hopes & merittes of the K[ing] were compard wth all his ancestors & it was prest as a preiudice therin if the grant should then be limitted, having beene absolut to the others. It was consented that a proviso should be added for the saving of those rightes: but in other things it was cravd wholie to be free, that the K[ing] might not thinke himself lessend in estimation. this argument was much forc't for the perswasion of the house, as after it was doubted to be elswher made their preiudice: but it prevail'd not against those other considerations that were rais'd, vpon/ wch it was concluded for a limitation & restraint.

the bill thus past that house had it's transition to the Lords, wher it receavd like favor & dispatch but was not made a lawe, wanting the *Roy le vuit*, wch being denied it, shewd what muft be look't for.

the next to this was the great question that was followd of the election made for yorkshire. it had from the first day o'th sitting beene in continuall agitation till that time. divers examinations & debates it had receavd in the Com^{tee}, severall reportes & motions in the house, a great disturbance it had beene to the whole business of either; a fierce spirit, it raisd almost in all the members. some in affection to the parties, who had drawne an inclination to their side, if it may be supposd in the integritie of that Court; & others in dislike of the practise that was vs'd. that by sharp argumentes, it had manie times beene handled, wch from the cause had now & then some sallies on the persons, & ther begatt distasts. the case, in short, was this. ther being a great emulation in the Countrie for that choise, a great concurse followd/ it at the Countie Court in yorke. the confusion being great, through the multitude of voices, ther was noe way of iudgment by the crie, & the venie was more vncertayne. the poll, wch is the touchstone in such cases, was the onlie means of triall; wch being demanded by Savill & his frinds, granted by the Sheriff, & follow'd in a part, was after interrupted & left off, & the iudgment & decision made wthout it. this was the case in breife, vpon wch it was obiected that the Sheriff was wholie Wentworth's, that he neglected in his favor, that dutie of his place to have proceeded in the poll, when he dif-

Page 81.

cernd & sawe Savill was like to carrie it; that being demanded it at first, wth much difficultie he admitted it, & pretended it a curtesie not a due. that contrarie to all right, having assum'd the iudgment to himself, he pronounc't the choise for Wentworth, wheras the other had more voices, double as was pretended. this suggestion & complaint, was fortified by certificat from the Countrie, vnder the hands of a hundred & fiftie of the freeholders & seven witnesses, *viva voce*, did attest it. infinit had beene the practifes/ of the others to decline this cause & question. divers delaies were vs'd to prevent it by the time. all the artes wch Northerne pollicie could invent to gaine advantage in the carriage, wch by the other were opposd wth noe less care & diligence, who, knowing those paths of subtiltie, followd the hunter in his trayne, & being more beaten to the waie, in his owne trap enfnar'd him. at the first hearing 'twas pretended by the Elect, that the complaint was onlie of the Sheriffe, & he therfore must iuftifie his fact. to that end was desir'd a time for his apparance to make his apologie & defence. that being granted [a] fortnight was spent therin for expectation of his comming, who affecting not the service, made noe hast. being at length convented, he answeard negatively to some things, dilatorilie to others, vncertainlie to all, that little truth could be gatherd from his words, less content & satiffaction from him self. he utterly denied Savill's pretence of voices, & on the contrarie affirmd, that in his iudgment theother had farr more. ffor the difficultie in granting of the poll, he excusd it by a reason of the time, & said it was past eleven before the demand was made. ffor the interruption he confest it was done as was alledg'd, five & thirtie/ being number'd it was proceeded in noe further: but the occafion he imputed vnto Savill, & that for two reasons. first wheras for the more perfitt carraage of the poll, the freehoulders wch were present at the reading of the writ, were all drawne into the caftell yard, & ther inclosd betweene the gates, those that were sworne & numbred being let out at the posterne, wch was done to avoid confusion and disorder & the abuse of such as might at severall times present themselves, & soe diverslie be reckon'd; Savill in this proceeding breaking open one of the Gates let in divers of his partie, that were newlie come & heard not the reading of the writ, who, as he thought had no interest in the election, but were a disturbance to the course and due order they were in. the second reason was that Savill raifing a report amongst the freeholders that the poll would last divers daies, gave therby such a difhartninge to the companie, as the gates before being open'd manie did depart for fear of long attendance; wch being knowne, he conceav'd it to be an interruption to the worke, vpon that left off the poll, & as in a case of much clearnefs as he thought on the behalf of Wentworth, both by the veiw & hearing/ he assumd the iudgment to him self; for confirmation of all wch he desir'd a new libertie for proofes. this againe made another protraction and delaye, wch was an advantage of some hope. the charge of ye prosecutor in attendance made some satiffaction in the pointe. the dailie increase o'th sicknefs shortned the expectation of the

o

sitting. all the imploimentes of the parliament were contracted for dispatch, wch promisd more then vsuall hast & brevitie, & therein was implied a possibilitie to preserve them. a high affection was difcernable in the pointe; & for this onlie was that prodigious motion the first daie. somuch corrupted are some harts in the sence of their perticulars as for their privat humors all publicke interefts are postposd. this delay being granted, brought forth nothing but another; when that libertie was expir'd, noe witnesses appeering for the Sheriff, the Elect then interposes for himself. libertie on his part was then requird also for defence, & a 'new time for witnesses, pretending great confidence in his right; and alledging, that the Sheriff, being faultie in his proofs, ought not to preiudice his cause, but as theother had, soe to him belongd a hearing./ much trouble this occasion'd in the deliberation of the house. some did obiect the cleerness of the proofe wch the other side had produc'd being affirmatlie & perticular. & that the poll being demanded in due time & interrupted by the Sheriff, though the maior part of voices might be doubtfull, was enough to avoid the election & returne, though it concluded not another; & therfore they might wth saftie pass to iudgment. others tp the interruption did alledge that the excuse was infufficient; for noe man was compellable to be present at the election, all had free libertie to depart. againe noe power might be supposd to force an interruption on a Sheriff, who had the whole power o'th Countie; therfore in that respect ther was noe reason to delay. Wentworth to this makes a protestation for himself, but by more heard then credited, that he affected not delaie in contemplation of himself, but defir'd onlie legallie to be heard, & that for the honor of the house. he vrg'd therfore, after a large narration of his cause, that it might be either granted or denied : if granted, that he might haue counsell to defend it; if otherwife, that by witnesses he might prove it, wch being the common rule of Justice, he expected in that Court & should/ therin accordinglie applie himselfe. this being seconded & enforc't, drew on an order for that time, that he should state his case in writing, deliver it to his adversarie, & he at the next sitting to give his answear thervpon. this though desir'd, was noe satiffaction vnto Wentworth, who came vnwillinglie soe neer the determination of the question, & that but to prevent the present decision wch he feard. he would faine haue kept at distance vpon the points of examination & defence : delaie and procraftination was his hope; manie things by that might occurr to worke his safetie; divers are the intervenients of time. the remotness of his witnefses was a faire pretext for this, if that occasion had beene granted him : but now that opportunitie depending vpon the difcreation of his adversarie, his hopes therin were lessen'd and what he had movd himself, himself againe repented. but the direction must be followd, & the case set downe in writing, wch being given to Savill, he foorthwth resorted to the house, & ther desir'd in some few things a hearing. being admitted, he made a short apologie for himself vpon the trouble of that cause, that it had soe long/ beene an interruption to their business.

Page 86.

Page 87.

that though he had small time for consideration of the case, as it was then in writing, it being deliverd him but late the night before; yet he did then accept it for conclusion of the worke, & to prevent their further trouble in the businefs. two things onlie he desir'd, that the paper wch was given him wth out name, might by his adversarie be subscribd; & that he might avowe, vpon his reputation in that house, somuch as concernd his knowledg to be true, & that the rest he thought soe. this begot new difficulties in Wentworth, who then suspected the issue of his artes; nothing he firſt doubted less then admission of his case, supposing the ielosie of his adversarie would haue made him fight at distance; but he that was his countriman and his equall, seeing the advantage readilie, closd presentlie vpon him in that grant & by concession of the case, surprisd & soe difarmd him. then againe he would haue flowen off to delaie & desird his witnesses might be heard to prove the pluralitie of voices, wch was denied him by the other. but the question being stated by himself, and that depending meerlie vpon the demand & interruption of the poll, the other was impertinent. wherfor his protestation was requird, wch though vnwillinglie/ was made, & the house went on to iudgment.

Page 88.

nothing did differ in this case from what was pretended by the Sheriffe. the interruption obiected vnto Savill was but vpon the rumor he gaue out, or for [from?] the opening of the gate. the demand supposd vnseasonable appeer'd otherwise by the proofes, & was implicitlie confest by the practise of the Sheriff, wheron some opinions being given that did declare against him, a new motion interpos'd for his councell to be heard, & soe diverted that course of resolution. much opposition was in this, the question being of fact; a great contestation it begott, even to the division of the house; vpon wch it being overrul'd, & the debate resum'd againe, a new interruption it receavd by a new motion for himfelf once more to be heard before they went to iudgment. great labor was for this, & as great care to stop it, intending but delaie. against him was obiected the long time he had had from the beginning of the Parliament, the often hearing he receavd att the Com^{tee}, in the house, wher his whole defence was knowne. that before he was wth drawne to give waie to the debate, as in all such cases it was vsuall, he had a full libertie to express himself, & his whole apologie was heard; / nothing could be added but protractation, wch would be a further iniurie to the house, & therfor was not to be admitted or receavd. vpon this it was soe resolvd, & the debate proceeded; when contrarie to the fundamentall orders of the house, by wch noe man may be present, at the agitation of his own cause, Wentworth came in confidentlie to his place, & gaue occafion to him that was then speaking to make this sallie on that fact, & from the question then in hand to reflect vpon the priviledg, wch thus was done for the preservation of that iewell.

Mr Speaker, the violation of our rightes may be well excusd by others, when they suffer violation by our selves. when our owne members practise it, when they shall doe it in contempt, in the heigth of scorne & iniurie, strangers and forreigners may be pardon'd,

Page 89.

who have ignorance to plead for them; all their attempts & actions being not soe preiudiciall as our owne.

if we admitt the dishonor of our selves, how then shall others value vs? & if we admitt a dishonor by our members, how/ shall we avoid it in ourselves? a greater dishonor and contempt this house has noe time suffred, then what does now affront it. to be excluded by a fundamentall order of the house, soe well knowne to all men, & that soe latelie vrg'd by him that now does breake it; to be debarrd on question, by a perticular act & rule, & yet to intrude against it, what is it less then to bid defiance to y^r power, & a farewell to y^r priviledge? should I compare it, it could have no paralell but that Roman's againſt whom Cicero does inveigh. *in senatum venit*, he comes into this Senat, but wth a will to ruine it; for soe I must interpret the intention of that act, that would deſtroie the priviledge. but did I say it was a member did it? I must retract that error in the place, or be fals to the opinion wch I have; for either by the election he pretends, or for this act & insolence, I cannot hould him worthie of that name, & soe, (involving both questions vnder one) as a full determination of his case, let/ vs from hence expell him.

this made him presentlie remov'd, & quickned the resolution of the house; wch for the interruption held the obiection to be frivilous; & for the demand, it was observd that the Sheriffe's act confirm'd it, besides the proofes that were produc'd, being affirmative, in the pointe; soe as the whole act of the Sheriff was condemned & thervpon the election adiudgd void; wch after somuch trouble & labor it had had, was the decision of that case. it may be wondred why we haue so farr travaild in this question, & in soe small a matter made soe perticular a relation; but it being the occasion of greater things to come, wee thought it not vnnecessarie the more carefullie to express it, that the power & influence may be seene of such small starrs, & planets, from whenc great workes, as Tacitus has observd, often receave originall. yet in the case it self, besides the art and carriage, the reason and decision are most profitable; for they doe shew what is the dutie in like cases, & how the vse directes it, that the poll in such elections being requir'd wthin the howers/ the statute does direct, wch is, from the reading of the writ, at anie time before eleven (for the printed books are falsified in that wch in figures make it *ix*, putting the *i* before the *x*, wheras the roll and originall has it otherwise, the *i* being following of the *x*) the poll soe demanded, noe pretence or interruption may excuse it: that all that come while the election is continuing though not present at the reading of the writ, haue their free votes & suffrage, wch shews the libertie of the Commons in the act of such elections, and the great care of Parliament to iustifie and preserve it, in w^{ch}, yet, noe man is compellable to attend. the maior part of Courtiers in this question banded maynlie against Wentworth, wherof he retaind a memorie; and others, that for pure reason did oppose him, he forgott not. the effect &

operation followd after of the sence he then contracted, wch from that sparke did rise to a great flame and burning. ther was in that gentleman a good choise of partes, naturall and acquisit, & noe less opinion of them. a strong eloquence he had, & a comprehension of much reason. his arguments were weightie & acute, & his defcriptions exquisit. when he would move his hearers/ wth the apprehension of his sence, he had both *acumina dictorum*, & *ictus sentiarum* to effect them. his abilities were great both in iudgment & perswasion, & as great a reputation did attend them. but those manie and great virtues, as Livie saies of Hanniball, as great vices paraleld, or rather they were in him as Cicero notes in Cataline, *signa virtutum*, formes of virtue onlie, not the matter; for they seldome were directed to good ends, & when they had that color, some other secret mov'd them. his covetousness & ambition were both violent, as were his waies to serve them. *neq̃ in pecunia, neq̃ in gloria concupiscenda*, as Crassus is render'd by Paterculus, *aut modum novit aut capiebat terminum*. & those affections rais'd him to somuch pride and choler, as anie opposition did transport him, wch render'd him less powerfull to his adversaries wher the advantage was follow'd and perceav'd.

Ther were two other cases of this nature, that had their determination about that time: one of Sr William Cope, who having beene a member of the former Parliament, in time of prorogation was arrested & taken in execution, & after, by *habeas corpus* going abroad, againe elected/ & return'd a burgess for Banburie. the question in this was double, whither he were w^{th}in the priviledg of Parliament in time of prorogation, & soe the arrest then void; & whither, being new chosen while he was in execution, the obiection should be good. both waies it was negativlie resolv'd. for the first, that the prorogation gives not priviledg, as an adiornment, further then the sixteene daies after for regress. for the second, that he being in execution was not eligible, bicause his enlargment would by lawe deprive the creditor of his debt. whervpon ther issued a warrant from the house for a new election to be made. the other case was of Mr Basset in Devonshire, who had two yeers beene a prisoner vpon originall & meane process arrefted for soe great a summe as noe man dar'd to bayle him, & being chosen a burgess for that Parliament was admitted & set free. I mention these cases to shew their different iudgmentes, & the rules of proceeding in that house, w^{ch}, as they are exact to preserve the publicke interestes, are curious also & instructive for the privat. iustice in all being the ground on wch they build, though the first stone & foundation be their priviledge./ Mountague at this time was attending, & cald to examination in the house, wher for the iustification of himself, he alledged a warrant of K[ing] J[ames] for the first booke he printed. that being sent for by the Archbishop, the K[ing] then tould him likewise, he should chuse whether he would goe to him or noe. that for his second booke, he had the like warrant & authoritie. that vpon the veiwe of his tenetes & opinions therin, the K[ing] swore, if that were to be a papist soe was he; whervpon he recommended

Page 95.

it to D^r. White, who by his censure did approve it, as was extant wth the worke. this confession being more confident then ingenuous begott new ielosies in the house; for his ould patron being dead, it could not be imagin'd he should assume that bouldness of him self. divers did wonder at it, who had fil'd their sails wth hope, & yet, difcernd not that the windes were turnd against them: but the more wise observ'd it as a constellation that was ominous, & therfore the more carefullie did studie to prevent it in the effectes. his bookes to this end were considered, wch had large matter of exception, besides the doctrines they implied/ (for the dispute of them, as noe fitt subiect for the Parliament, the wisdome of the Commons did decline) besides his innovations in the doctrine, wch for another censure was reserv'd. divers of scandall were deduc'd, to the diſhonor of the K[ing], the disturbance of the State, both for the church & goverment, & in derogation of the Parliament, for contempt of the priviledge & iurifdiction of that house, & in preiudice of the whole. instances were cited in all these. & first for dishonor to the K[ing], his vphoulding the opinions of Arminius was observ'd, which the K[ing] labord somuch to suppress; wch labor was apparent in three maine actes & principles;

first, by his writings, in wch he termes Arminius an enemie to God, & Bertius his scholler, for his booke, *de apostasia sanctorum,* an hereticke; secondlie, by procuring the Synod at Dort, & favoring & approving their decrees, at wch his owne divines assisted; thirdlie, by sending the articles of the Church of England into Ireland, vnder the

great seale & teste & to the 38th of iustifying faith, wher it
is said that it cannot be lost, adding for explanation (totallie
& finallie) wch was intended in the sence & meaning/ of Page 97.
the article, by all wch he indeavor'd the suppressing of those
doctrines wch the writings of Arminius would bring in,
therfore the contrarie, wch by Mountague was affected, infer'd a dishonor to the K[ing].

the second pointe of disturbanc in the church & state
in fower particulars was collected. first his sowing of
ielosies betweene the K[ing] & his good subiectes, terming
the puritans (whom he defin'd) to be a potent prevailing
faction in the kingdome. secondlie his slighting those
famous divines, who have beene great lightes in the church,
Calvine, Beza, Perkins, Whitakers, thirdlie, his laboring to
discountenanc the ministrie of God's word, terming the
Lectures, by way of Ironie & scorne, propheticall determi-
nations & conventicles; preaching prating, & the like.
fourthlie, his giving incouragment to Poperie, & a perswa-
fion thervnto, affirming Rome to be a true church, & the
spous of Christ. all wch was noted to intend sedition &
disturbanc. the third generall of derogation to the Parliament, & the iurisdiction of that house, was thus infer'd.
first, that being vnder examination & complaint ther for
his former booke, he publisht the second in/ defenc & Page 98.
maintenance of the same. & then that in that second he
did scandall & revile those that did prosecute on the first,
who in that respect were in the protection of that house,
& could not therin be calumniated wthout violation of the
priviledge. these observations produc'd these motions &

desires. first that ther might be a charge prepar'd against him, out of the matter then propounded to be tranfmitted to the Lords. then, that he might, in the meane time be committed for his contempt & iniurie to the house, & soe remayne a prisoner wth the Sariant vntill his further punishment. these opinions, though most agreeing wth the house, had yet some opposition & resistance. it was first obiected against the authoritie of the house, that one Parliament had not cognisance of another, nor were the offences to a former questionable, much less punishable in a latter: but the vanitie of that argument was discoverd by the cleer light of reason & authoritie; the whole course of Parliament spake against it, the practise of all times, the examples of all Courtes. divers presidents were cited for illustration in the point/ wch soone compos'd that question. others that had an inclination to that partie (for even wth Christ ther was one Judas in the fellowship) obiected the nature of the cause & by making it seeme doctrinall would exclude the iurifdiction of that Court; & for the doctrines likewise labord to insinuat a defenc, for that they were not by anie publicke act condemnd in the censure of the church: but these assoone were reiected & cast off by differenc & distinction of the fact, in that the pointes infifted on were but civill, for the honor of the K[ing], the priviledg of the Parliament, the peace & quiet of the State, the virtue & tranquilitie of the church, wch it was said, by ffleta were appropriat to the secular Courtes & magistrats. these reasons were a satisfaction to that doubt. but further it was added, that the articles being oppos'd wch were confirm'd by Parliament, the Parliament ought in dutie to maintaine them, vpon wch it was wth out difficultie resolvd both for the Commitment & the charge, & Mountague being cald in, kneeling at the barr, had, for his contempt, a censure of commitment/ ther pronunc't. Some by waie of caution had propounded a cunctation in that act, for the honor of the house, least, contrarie to their meaning, it should prove, for a punishment, a preferment: but that reason was thought lighter then the rest; wch the effect & consequenc prov'd true, & was not punicke, as twas thought, but reall & by a right inspection of the time; nor that by revelation but by iudgment truelie taken from the meridian of the State, wch had that infortunitie wth others, to make men most obnoxious most secure, and those that were most hatefull to the publicke, to be most honor'd & esteem'd.

Hitherto all things had succeeded to the intentions of that house, noe interruptions had beene raisd by the influenc of State. those few publicke things then treated of, had a free way of preparation, though some intimations had beene given that their conclusions would not answeare it, but those had less in credit, then of truth, and the satiffaction was presum'd to be equall to the hope. from the confidence of Mountague & that businefs, some seedes of ielosie/ were emergent, but noe more. all things els had a sure shew & promise. the bill of tonnage & pondage was at rest in the custodie of the Lords, & noe knowledg, but by divination could be had, how it would speed after wth the K[ing]. the best was still expected as hope did make construction, wch alwaies has an inclination vnto flatterie.

But heer a checke came in, as distractive as vnlook't for. the D[uke of Buckingham] who was the Eolus of that time, had cast an alteration in the aer; the windes were turnd, & all the former happinefs must be shadow'd wth some new clouds & vapors he had rais'd. he comes from the K[ing], who was then at Hampton Court, wth a pretended order for a new motion of supply. this in all hast must be performd & his privado's were all sent for to receave instruction in the pointe. this was about twelve a clock at night, at his owne house, wher, by reason of the suddainnefs & vnseasonableness of the time, manie were not present, nor such as had much iudgment, they commonlie being most attendant on such persons, who are/ most obnoxious to their humors. these did confent in all, who studied not to counfell but to please; & soe what affections he had brought, they did both heigthen & confirme. but in the morning when it was come to others, whose qualitie was more knowing and ingenuous, they, as they apprehended it to be fatall & prodigious, soe gave it demonstration to the D[uke]. & wth all their power oppos'd it, adding to argumentes, entreaties for the prevention of that evill, wch did impplie apparantlie dishonor to the K[ing], [&] danger to him. of this number (not to deprive anie man of his due) was Sr Humphry May, then Chancelor of the Dutchie, who, having travaild wth much industrie in that service, but in vaine, came in great hast to a gentleman whom he thought more powerfull wth the

D[uke] & knew to be affectionat to the publicke, & him he importund to a new attempt & triall for staie or diversion of that worke. it was at Westminster wher he mett him, & neer the time of the sitting of the Commons. the D[uke] was then at York house. the entercourse/ 'twas obiected, would be long. noe certaine period could be prescribd for conference, wch in soe great a difficultie was not likelie to be short; soe as the proposition to the Parliament might be made before the discourse were ended, & the travaile by that means fruitless and vnnecessarie. but to remove this doubt the chancelor vndertooke to stop the motion till he came. onlie he wisht him to hasten his returne, & in his talke to intimat that staie vnto the D[uke]. vpon this he makes his passage & address, & comming to York house, findes the D[uke] wth his Ladie yet in bed; but notice being given of his comming, the Dutchess rose & w^thdrew into her cabanett, & soe he was foorthw^th admitted & lett in. the first thing mention'd was the occasion, & the fear that was contracted from that ground. the next was the honor of the K[ing] & respect vnto his saftie, from both wch were deduc'd argumentes of disswasion. ffor the king's honor was rememberd, the acceptation that was made of the two subsidies wch were past, & the satiffaction then profest, wch the new proposition would impeach, either in truth or wisdome, &/ againe the small number of the Commons that remaynd, the rest being gone vpon the confidenc of that overture, would render it as an ambuscado & surprise; wch at noe time could be honorable towardes subiectes, less in the en-

Page 103.

Page 104.

trance of the Soveraigne. the rule for that was noted, *ut initia proveniant fama in ceteris est.* the necessitie likewise of that honor was observ'd, wthout wch noe prince was great, hardlie anie fortunat. & on these grounds a larger superstructure was imposd as occasionallie the conferenc did require. ffor his owne saftie, manie things were said, some more fitt for vse, then for memorie & report. the generall disopinion was obiected, wch it would worke to him, not to have oppos'd it, whose power was knowne to all men; & that the command comming by him self, would render it as his act, of wch imputation what the confequence might be nothing but divinitie could iudge, men that are much in favor being obnoxious to much envie. To these, answears were returned though weake, yet such as implied noe yeelding, that the acceptation wch was made of the subsidies then granted, was but in respect of/ the affection to the K[ing], not for satiffaction to his business. that the absence of the Commons was their owne fault & error, & their neglect muſt not preiudice the State. that the honor of the K[ing] stood vpon the expectation of the ffleet, whose designe would vanishe if it were not speedilie set foorth. monie ther was wanting for that worke, & therin the king's honor was ingag'd, wch must outweigh all considerations for himself. this resolution being felt, was a new waie attempted, to trie if that might weaken it. & to that end was obiected the improbabilitie of success; & if it did succeed, the greater loss might follow it, by alienation of the affections of the subiectes, who being pleasd were a fountaine of supplie, wthout wch those streames would soone drie vp. but nothing could prevaile, ther being divers argumentes spent in that, yet the proposition must proceed, w^{th}out consideration of success, wherin was lodg'd this proiect, meerlie to be denied. this secret that treatie did discover, wch drew on/ others that supported it Page 106. of greater weight & moment, shewing a conversion of the tide for the present. it gave that gentleman some wonder wth astonishment, who wth the seale of privacie clos'd vp those passages in silence, yet therin grounded his observations for the future that noe respect of persons made him desert his countrie.

this labor, not mispent, had taken vp much time. two houres, at least, went into the treatie & discourse, wch wth the entercourse had soe wasted the forenoone as ther remayn'd but little at his comming backe to Westminster; wher the like difficultie had beene to retard the proposition for that time, it being putt (not as other messages from the K[ing] into the mouth of his councellors and great officers, wherof ther are neuer wanting in the Commons house too manie; but) by a speciall choise, to the difcreation of another, as an indication of his preferment then at hand, who was great, in his opinion, wth that honor & imploiment, & labor'd, as a woman does wth child, in desire to bring it foorth. the success being ther/ imparted, the Page 107. motion did proceed. for wch ther wanted not some fitness in that instrument. the man so chosen was Sr John Coke, raisd from a lowe condition to that title by the D[uke]. to him he had beene recommended by that ould courtier S^r ffoulke Grevill, vnder whom he had had his education as a scholler, & soe was his service & imploiment; but his conversation being wth bookes, & that to teach not studie them, men & business were subiectes wch he knew not, & his expressions were more proper for a schoole, then for a State & councell. this choise, thus fitted, thus made his entrance to that sceane, that the K[ing] not doubting their affections in that meeting, & taking gratiouslie for a testimonie therof the guift wch was resolved on, as a welcome pledge of the love, not onlie of that representative bodie of the kingdome, but of the whole (though he tooke notice of their anticipation in that businefs, & that they fell into it w^thout the intervention of anie ministers of State, wch he did impute to their forwardness in his service, & confidence in his favor) in correspondence

Page 108. therof/ had commanded him to give the house a true information of his estate, & to laie before them the necessities he was in. that ther had lately beene disburst for Ireland to confirme the peace of that kingdome—32000^li, for the Navie (the present preparations not computed—37000^li & for the office of the ordinance & fforts—47000^li, for the support of the regimentes in the Lowe Countries—99000^li, for the charge of Count Manffeilts armie—62000^li & because from that last business had growne some doubtes, he was to give a more perticular accompt therin. his late Matie loving peace, & hating warr, when he sawe how ill he had beene vs'd, that the power of the contrarie partie had almost overpowrd christendome, & his owne people discontented at his seeming backwardness in that cause ; considering the three subsidies & fifteenths

that were granted him, though a roiall guift, would onlie
enable him for awhile to secure his owne, & that in the
end, he should growe, from a lingring ague, to a burning
feaver, & by suffring his enemies to enioye that wch they
had gotten, make them more able by degrees to frett vpon
the other/ German princes, whenc it would ensue, that Page 109.
like Vlisses wth Polypheme, he should onlie have the favor
to be the last devour'd, he negotiated & concluded a strong
confederacie wth the K. K. of ffrance & Denmarke, the
state of Venice, the D[uke] of Savoy, & the Low Countries, wch first appeerd in the armie beyond the Alpes, and
wth Count Manffeilt. some faultes he said, were to be
confest in those troopes at Dover, wch could not be excus'd,
but Manffeilt complaind that the men were chosen such as
would be kept vnder noe goverment. & if it were obiected
why a stranger should lead those troopes; it was to be
considered, that the whole armie did consift of English,
ffrench, & Dutch, & if an Englishman had commanded it
the ffrench would have been discontented, & soe the English
if a ffrenchman; & if manie commanders had beene made,
precedenc would have bred some difficulties; therfore he
that was indifferent was thought to be the fittest. & if a
further obiection be taken from the event, it must be
likewise confidered that noe success is man's, & he that
measures/ things by that is noe equall iudge. he said also it Page 110.
was true, that the change of the designe caused some delaie,
& impeachment of that good effect wch was hoped; yet it
was not altogeather vnprofitable, for the apparanc of that
armie kept divers princes of Germanie from diclaring them

selves for the enemye. this was in generall as he said, towardes the accompt of the three subsidies & fifteenths. & further his ma^{tie} had commanded him to give an accompt of that wch would be spent vpon the preparation then in hand. the charge of the ffleet in the office of the Navie—200000^{li}, in the office of the ordinance—48000^{li}, for the landmen it would be—45000^{li} wherof the two subsidies then given would amount to but—160000^{li}. but this not all. the K[ing] of Denmarke was to have—40000^{li} to draw him into Germanie, befides a monthlie entertainment of—20000^{li} & asmuch to Count Manffeilt, wch could not be supported wth out help of Parliament, or els some new waie; the ordinarie revenew being exhausted & ouercharg'd wth other expences both of necessitie & honor. that the K[ing]/ when he was prince borrowed—20000^{li} for these provisions. the Lord Admirall hath ingag'd his estate. other ministers haue furnisht above—50000^{li}. shall it be said that these men are left to be vndone for their readinefs to the publicke services? shall we proclaime our owne povertie by loofing all that is beftowed vpon this enterprise, bicause we cannot goe through wth it? what shall we say to the honor of the K[ing]? but that is not all, even the establishment of his ma^{tie} in his roiall throne; the peace of chriftendome, the state of religion, depend vpon this ffleet. the adversaries deliuer verie insolent speeches ever since the taking of Breda. the ffrench encline to civill warr; they brandle in Italie, & faint as their forefathers were wont to doe after the heat of the first enterprise. our German forces haue kept the Catholick league from assembling to the ruine of the protestantes. what have we to revnite the princes, to encourage the ffrench, to support the States, to oppose the Catholicke League, but the reputation of Manffeilt's armie, & the expectation of our ffleet? shall/ it be said that being forsaken Page 112. of his subiects the K[ing] hath beene enforc't to abandon religion? to seeke a dishonorable peace? it is impossible for these things to subsist but by monie, or credit. thus spake that worthie, & then concluded wth this motion, that either they would presentlie make an addition of supplie, or pass some ingagement to the K[ing], that at the next meeting they would doe it; wch might give him credit in the interim, & soe the expedition to goe on. this motion had noe second, but by Beecher a councell clarke & servant of that time; but his reason & authoritie being not great, & all the other Courtiers disaffecting it, being in briefe oppos'd by a worthie gentleman of Lincolnshire Sr Thomas Grantham, who was never wanting to the service of his countrie, it forthwth died & perisht, though from the dust thereof more troubles did spring vp. the frame & composition of that bodie, was thought as preposterous as the sowle; the immense calculations & accomptes, & the far fetch't & impertinent relations; the positions and conclusions that were laid, all held artificiall & prestigious. his/ supposition of their forsaking of the K[ing] & the Page 113 King's abandoning religion, was deemd both scandalous & offensive; as was that mention of new waies, wch the more was noted, bicause it had happen'd once before, & therfore was not thought to be accidentall or by chance:

but exceptions were declin'd, through the wisdome of that time, w^ch, in the dying of that motion had satisfaction & content. ther was noe deniall, nor noe question, it being never brought soe farr, wch had almost a miracle w^thin it; for ther were hardlie then threescore in the house, & of those, countrimen not the most. anie support or agitation it had had must have needs driven it to a concession, or the contrarie; but, as we noted, the Courtiers much difliking it, some as it came not in perticular by them, or that they were not preconsulted for the worke; others for the danger & preiudice it imported; the rest for the suddenness & strangeness of the thing, that like a lightinge brake vpon them, having noe precogitation of the meteor; all generallie abhorring it, as a constellation that was ominous,/ it vanisht through it's owne lightnefs & futilitie, causing a reluctation in their hartes, wch nothing but divinitie could move. this vnexpected issue to the D[uke] caus'd a new trouble & diforder. all his privado's were condemn'd, as remiss & negligent in the service. his frindes were all complain'd of, thus to haue fail'd his hopes. everie man was blam'd but him that was most faultie. what he intended in his corrupt reason, or affection, to that he would have had even the heavens themselves confenting. soe vnhappie are such persons, through the distractions of their greatness, that success the[y] thinke to follw the *Via Lactea* of their fancies, & that the rule of that, naie of the world it self, should be by the proportion of their willes. & rather then faile them, if the superiors be not flexible, the infernall powers shalbe studied, wth their artes. this was the infelicitie of this man, & at this time it first open'd & difcover'd, though not cleerlie but by shadows, being disorderd in their purpose, wch almoſt noe man yet did know, he condemns both his ffortune & his frindes: but for himself nothing was/ less resolvd on, then that wch was most necessarie. noe retraction of the course. that wch had beene, because it was done by him, muſt be both iuſtified & maintain'd, & that iustification must appeer in the approbation of the worke by a future prosecution that was worse.

the house being delivered from the fear, wch it had contracted from that motion, & the consequence that might followe it, forthwth resolv'd to think of nothing but recess, & the next daie intimated their readiness to the Lords, who having dealt in little at this meeting, & having noe business at that time, dispatcht a present messenger to the K[ing], from whom they receavd this answear, that though his necessities were great, yet the consideration of their safties should dispose him to dismiss them for that time, though they must shortlie meet againe.

that shortlie, was not then rightlie vnderſtood. noe man did doubt that wch the word intended. most men did refer it to the Winter or the Spring, the conventions of that Councell/ being seldome neerer, or more frequent : but an effect it was of the powerfull influenc of the D[uke] wch not long after was more' perspicuous & apparant. both by that latter clause of the answear, & the rest, all men did know that their sitting was not long, & therfor sought to state their business in some order. the cheife care was for preservation of the statutes wch stood vpon continuance to that time. for this a short act was fram'd, that the roiall assent, should not (as was supposd by some, though presidents spake the contrarie) give a determination to that session; but that it should continue by adiornment, & all things stand in the condition that they left them, soe to be resum'd againe at the next time of meeting. this done, & the act of confirmation being past for three subsidies then granted by the clergie, ther being a little time remayning, it was spent vpon a petition from the prisoners in the ffleet. they had beene suitors to the Lords, in respect of the great danger of the sickness, to have libertie by order from the Parliament, by *habeas corpus* to goe abroad. the Lords imparted/ this motion to the Commons. the Commons thervpon taking consideration at this leasure, vpon these reasons thus resolv'd it to be repugnant to the lawe. first that it was against the intention of the writt, wch commanding the keeper to bring his prisoner to a Judge, implies the neerest waie he has, not as the abuse went, to let him travell wher he list, to hunte & hawke the whole vacation in his countrie, & at terme againe to resort vnto his prison. then that it was legallie an escape, & soe the creditors should be preiudiced; for wch ther were divers iudgmentes cited, & some cases demonstrative in the pointe, as 5° H[enry] 6. when in confideration of the state, ther being speciall service at that time for some minifter then imprison'd, & the like libertie was defird, the Judges, vpon consultation, did denie it. & before that, it was noted, that all kinde of ease or remove from one prison to another, was wholie refus'd, wthout consent & liking of the creditors. for this, therfore, it being soe contrarie to the lawe, & in favor of abuse, howeuer pittie did move in contemplation of the men, yet their dangers being not equall to the danger of the/ kingdome, wch would followe the exin- Page 118. anition of the lawes, it was thought fit, not in that perticular to admitt it, or that admission, at the least, not to be made by Parliament; wch opinion being signified to the Lords, they in like manner did resolve it, & soe all instance [insistence?] ceast. this was the ninth of Julie being Saturdaie. on moundaie ther was a message to the Commons from the Lords to intimat their receipt of a Commission of adiornment, & another for the roiall assent to the passage of some lawes, for wch their presenc was desird in the Lords house, as it was alwaies in such cases, to hear them read. vpon this some short disputes arising in consideration of their priviledg, they resolv'd them, wth what brevitie they might & soe made ther passage to that end. the first difficultie was for presenting the bill of subsidie; the vsuall manner being, that that having past the Lords, should be return'd againe as the peculiar of the Commons, & when they attended, either for dissolution or adiornment, as their free act, to be presented by their Speaker: this being then not done, rais'd some ielosie in the pointe, least it might draw a preiudice in the future, both on their affecting & those acts: but being then annext to the Commission for assent, wth theother lawes to pass, & that Commission/ resting properlie wth the Lords, it was conceav'd Page 119. that ceremonie could not be, but the Speaker must supplie

R

it, in an expression at the place, & ther receave & deliver it in their names. the next was the confideration of the adiornment wherin likewise some little doubt ther was for their interest in that pointe, wch having alwaies beene their owne sole act & worke, in admitting it by commission from the K[ing], it was then thought an innovation of the right, wch might induce a president against them, & soe retrench their libertie for the future. & for this purpose the difference was observd betweene adiornment & prorogation, as prorogation & dissolution have their odds. that the two latter, in their kindes, were in the prerogative of the K[ing], the adiornment, in the priviledge onlie of the hovse. therfore a message in that case was dispatch't for accommodation wth the Lords; who thervpon agreed to read onlie in their presence the Commission for assent, & in theother to leave them wholie to themselves. all things thus settled & compos'd, the Commons did address themfelves to hear the Commission of assent, &/ being present wth the Lords, & the Speaker ther receaving the bill of subsidie in his handes, as it was hanging wth the others to the Commission that must pass them, vsing some rhetoricke in the diclaration of their right, & by their affection in the guift making an insinuation to the K[ing] in the name of all the Commons, he presented it; wch had acceptance by the Keeper, & this anfwear thervpon. that the K[ing] apprehended it as a good testimonie of their loves, & in correspondency of that would enlarge his favor to his subiectes. that in their peitie & religion, he would meet them; & for their petition therin given him, the answear should be reall & not verball. that they should shortlie haue a perticular satiffaction in that pointe, & in the meane time, he would command a strick't execution of the lawes. wherevpon the roiall assent being read for the enacting of some bills, wherof the subsidie was not least in estimation & accompt; & the king's pleasure intimated for an adiornment vnto Oxford, the attendanc did dissolve, & the Commons returnd vnto their house, noe less affected wth trouble, then admiration, the suddainness of the time, being but the first of August, & that the eleventh of / Julie, wch was an exposition of that misterie, that formerlie was mistaken, & an explication of the meaning of that word shortlie, & much more; this, with the strangeness of the place, both vnexpected & vnlook't for, seem'd as a prodigie to all men. the vnaptnefs of the season for such a concourse & assemblie, wch was scarcelie safe at anie time but moft dangerous then, in that the epedemicall infection of the plague being soe vniversallie disperst, that all persons were suspected & in ielosie, men, if they could, even flying from themselves; the houses, streets & waies, naie euen the feilds & hedges, almost in all places neer London & about it (besides the miserable calamities of the citie) presenting dailie new spectacles of mortalitie. the place also was noted, as something ominous & portentous, for the success it gave to the like meetinge in foretimes. it rais'd a contemplation of the miseries wch followd that vnfortunat convention in the daies of H[enry] 6. wth the reasons & intentions that had mov'd it ; & from the resemblance of the causes was deduc'd a like supposition of the effects, w^{ch}/ gaue a fear to all men, who in their hartes

Page 121.

Page 122.

deplor'd the vnhappinefs of those princes that expose themfelves to the corruption of their ministers. to sharpen that humor & dislike, at that time happened also the infection of that place. it was entred into some few houses of the towne, & some of the Colledges were infected. most of the schollers were retir'd, & that was an aggravation to the danger; w[ch] being apprehended to the full, became an aggravation of the fear, by w[ch] that fact (though a iustice in the K[ing]) was thought an iniurie in his servantes. but obedience was resolv'd on, & through all the difficulties of the time, the king's pleasure was prefer'd. the Lords vpon the departure of the Commons from their house, read ther the Commission for adiornment (somuch they differ from theothers in order, or observation) who having likewise the writt brought downe to them, refus'd to read or open it. but as their owne act, not varying in the circumstance, pronounc'd it by ther Speaker, that the Howse adiorn'd it self, & soe dissolved that meeting.

Page 123.   The report of this flew presentlie to all partes/ & affected all men wth wonder at the strangenefs. London was then the constant seat of Parliamentes, w[ch] noe wher els had beene for divers ages past, that in the vulgar sence they were incorporat to that place. the time likewise seem'd a miracle to those who had retir'd themfelves, being members of that bodie, & heard the acceptation of their subfidies in the message from the K[ing] the complement that was in it, for respect vnto their safties, endeard by high expressions of comparison, was also in their memories. the incongruitie wth that, in this alteration & adiornment, wrought much anxietie in their thoughtes, &, as farr as fear could carrie it, made a depression of their hopes. this all men had for their entertainment in the countrie during that short recess. some had but opportunitie, whose habitations were remote, to make onlie a visit to their families & at first sight to leave them. hardlie anie one had leasure for their fit accommodation & provisions, but suffered some inconvenience or defect. their trauell on the waies, their danger in the Inns, & the little saftie could be/ promisd at the period, tooke off all pleasure from the iorney ; & the occasion that did move it was more distastfull then the rest. the satisfaction had at London was not much, the promise then farr less. ther in the matter of religion, though ther were a faire answear in the generall yet Mountague was protected, & to that end made chaplaine to the K[ing]. in other things the answear to the greivances was but slight, & such as imported small fruite to the subiect. the bill of tonnage & pondage was reiected & yet those levies made ; wch was held an indication of more love to the waies of power then right. the lawes that had their approbation were not manie & the choise of them not great. that against recusantes was not past, & in all, their number was but seven, whereof the subsidies of the laitie & clergie made vp two, soe as the rest imported little to publicke happiness, as their following titles may express.

1. An Act for punishing of divers abuses committed on the Lord's daie.
2. An Act to enable the K[ing] to make leases in the Dutchie of Cornwall.

3. An Act for ease in obteining licences of alienation.

4. An Act for restraint of Alehouses & victualing houses.

5. An Act for confirmation of the subsidies granted by the clergie.

6. An Act for two entire subsidies granted by the temporaltie.

7. An Act, that the session should not then determin by the roiall assent to other Actes.

that for religion, for soe it was pretended; onlie did provide against bul baitings, enterludes, & the like vnlawfull pastimes on the Sundaie. & therin alſo, wth a mixture of civill considerations & respectes.

that for the Dutchie had aspect but to the profit of the K[ing], though wth some shadowe & pretence of advantage to the tenantes. that for alienations onlie lookt at some small decrease of fees, & had reference but to few, & rarelie of vse to them. that for restraint of Alehouses was, in effect, but what had beene before, for the repressing of tiplings & disorders, wch both before & then were more decried then punished, as reformation is less easie then complaint. the rest need not comment to explaine them, sence wthout/ reason, making demonstration of the subsidies; & for the other, if it had wanted midwives, much trouble had beene sav'd, wch afterwardes did followe that prodigious birth, at Oxford.

ILLUSTRATIVE ADDITIONS
FROM
SIR JOHN ELIOT'S UNPUBLISHED MSS.
AT PORT ELIOT.

SUPPLEMENT.

PROPOSE to redeem my promise (in the 'Introduction' and elsewhere) to give from other MSS. at Port Eliot such Speeches of Sir John Eliot as in the earlier, were doubtless worked into the lost *Negotium Posterorum* 'Tomus Primus,' and in the later, fill vp the summaries and notices of *Negotium Posterorum* 'Tomus Secundus.' The MSS. are numerous and weighty; for the Patriot was as industrious in collecting and transcribing authorities and 'precedents' and his reading was as wide as his friend Sir Robert Cotton's. I necessarily confine myself to such as are still of *quick* and personal interest. I proceed from the commencement of the precious volume on and on to the close, following the pencil-marked folios of Mr. Forster, who arranged them for the binder.

First of all we have Sir John Eliot's first speech in the House of Commons, 'Anno 21°. Jacob. reg.' Parliament met on the 12th of February, 1623-4, but was adjourned to the 19th. On the 27th business began in the Commons. Three, or at most four days thereafter Sir John Eliot made the first speech of the Session. There were time-servers and Facers-both-ways who would have kept silence on the King's recent misdoings, even have entered into compacts with Buckingham. Eliot would not be muzzled, nor have 'understandings.' "He must therefore," says Forster, "raise his voice for those favours their ancestors had enjoyed; and it is memorable that he should thus have spoken his first speech in the House elaborately to defend those parliamentary immunities and rights for which afterwards he suffered death" (vol. i. p. 135).

Folios 2-6.
A speach in Parliament.
A°. 21°. Jacob reg.

"M^r Sp^r.

Wee cannot but remember the antient opinions held of those assemblies, and how happie theire effects haue beene vnto this kingdome; how like a Sanctuarie they haue beene ever to ye subiects, how like a magazine to the princes: the princes heer for the most part granting such lawes and reformacons as were covenable for the necessities and welfare of theire Subiects, and the Subiects, to reciprocat the affeccons of theire princes, often making there retribucons larger then was expected: but in the two last Conventions, at one of wch I was present, and to the other a wellwisher, wherein ye necessities of the Kinge and Countrie mutuallie sought for the interchaing of helpe and assistance from each other; The home and forayne occasions of the Kinge and State requiring Supplie and aide from the Countrie: the wants and greevances of the Countrie vrging releif and remedie from the Kinge. When on both sides there was most expected, most needed, and the King most gratiouslie began to offer himselfe to the Subiects in all things befitting a mercifull and pious prince, and the Subiects againe returninge theire thanckfullness wth extraordinary demonstrations to the Kinge : in these I say (o^h that I could not saie in these last meetings) miserie crept into the place of happiness and by ielosies and distraccōns tooke from vs the benefitt of those Counsells, wch hope had made equall to the wisedome of o^r Elders.

Vpon these I knowe not what opinions wee should now retaine, whether the meetings be the same they were, and only differ in the effects, or that the times haue chang'd the reason and soe brought it to a new forme, wch how it may agree wth the safetie and hono^r of this State & Countrie as I am ignorant, I should be glad to learne. It was the character of a wiseman in the last age, vpon this point, that the greatest vnhappines could befall this kingdome was that o^r Parliaments should become imperfect ; and that the dissent here betweene the Prince and people was the most dangerous ; wch how it hath of late beene *quanquā animus meminisse horret*, as that wherein the Soule of this kingdome hath already too much suffered ; yet give me leave I beseech yo^u a little to review it, that wee may then studie an easier way for o^{r}selues. *faciunt aliena pericula cautos* ; and its a cheape way of learninge vpon the costs of other men.

Somethings wee shall finde in the Kinge, some things in our selues, that may occasion these breaches : if either thorough diffidence in his Matie, ielosie amongst o^r selues, or vnsecresie in our businesse, wee goe a troubled way : for the distrust of a Soueraigne is euer as disadvantagable, as the hate of an Enemie, and where wee are not confident of our selues what can wee expect from others; it cannot be, but inconveniencies will follow where they are not prevented, therefore, I shall earnestly desire before yo^u discend into any pticuler disputes, y^t you will a littell reflect vpon this generall, what hath beene, and from thence consider what may now be done.

In the former of the two last vnfortunate assemblies, as I remember, there was an aspersion of vndertaking cast vpon the service of some members of the howse, from whence there grew a ielosie in the rest, that the whole busines, was compounded by those principalls, whoe had before hand given the Kinge assurance of what he desired : this ielosie being entred into a parte, like a canckrous vlcer spread wth the sharpness of it's owne corrupt humor, and by infection went soe farr as it diseaséd the body : the bodie being once sick & ill affected could not presently finde a remedy, or remove the cause, but by continuance of the greif had the symptomes more dangerous then the disease : for from the roote of that ielosie sprange vp opposition & contestation in debates : opposition branch't it selfe to faction : faction (or rather fraction I might call itt) offten budded and put forth personall quarrells not only to the publique preiudice but detracting from the honor and gravitie of this soe great and graue a Senate : and all this moved by the aere and breath of that vnknowne & vaine report of vndertakers :

whereas I verilie beleeue there was noe such thinge in ye King's hart by secrett practise wth a few to vndermyne the rest, nor would those few for themselues assume somuch power aboue others to vndertake for all; but that o^r ielosie in this case was the advantage of the ill affected, who made it the instrument of theire designes to dissolve that meetinge, that they might follow their owne proiects & inventions then on foote, which (as wee haue since felt) trencht more vpon the priviledges & liberties of this kingdome then the vttermost vndertaking in Parliament can ever doe.

In the last meetinge it were presumption in me that have nothing thence but on creditt, to make soe neere a search or censure only of the effect: yo^u will pardon me to complayne whoe lost some hopes in that publique adventure.

I feare (M^r Sp^r.) the rocks were not naturall on wch yo^u then stroke but cast in the waie by some subtill arte to prevent the passage of y^r duties to the Kinge: neither can I thinke the intercourse was more easie for his Maties love to yo^u; but that by oblique windes, & tides his Graces were sometimes diverted, or preiudicate: this I am most confident of, both concerning his Matie and the howse, that never king wth more gracious resolutions for the comfort & benefitt of his Subiects Call'd a Parliam^t; nor subiects wth more sinceare affections came devoted to theire Prince, but in this doubtless there was some misprision, and betweene his Matie and the howse stood some fals glasses, that reflected not the trew sence of the obiect, but wth colors and illusions wrought deceipte.

The greatest doubts (as I conceive) the kinge had of the Parliam^ts concerned his prerogative; his Matie being perswaded that theire liberties did intrench vppon him. the feares the Parliaments had of the Kinge were that by his prerogative he sought to retrench & block vp the antient priviledges & liberties of the house. this made the insistance stronge on both sides, the Kinge mayntayneing his royall power: the howse pretendinge for their priviledges, whereas, being well distinguish't both might freely haue enioyde theire owne w^thout impeachment of the others right: ffor the Kings prerogative noe man may dispute against it, it being an inseperable adiunct to regalitie, and exampled in the first, and greatest monarck, the Kinge of Kinges, who reserves to himselfe beyond his lawes a power to save wch Seneca calls *proprium regis*, & we his prerogative.

ffor the priviledges of Parliam^t. they have beene such & soe esteemed, as neither detract from the hono^r of the kinge nor lessen his authoritie, but conduce to the libertie of this place, that wee may heere freely treate and discourse for the publique good of the kingedome, wch I take to be a maine bass and prop whereby it doth subsist: for as the Parliam^ts haue beene ever held to be the cheife support and piller of the kingedome soe is this priviledge of the Parliam^ts by wch opinions are plainelie delivered, difficulties beaten out, & truth resolued vpon; whereas otherwise men fearinge to displease will blanch those propositions that may haue question; and silence theire vnderstandings in matters of most importe. & in this the protestacon last made, gives me greate satisfaccon as proceeding from Excellent deliberations, and advise. & the reasons being well weighed (besides the habit & longe vse of this place wch hath still been held wth greate regarde to the hono^r, & dignitie of the head ye kinge) the reasons I say may induce the allowance and consent : the business is the Kings, the kingdome is the Kings, the resolucons rest wholie in ye Kinge, and wee are only called hither by the Kinge, either vpon the generall affaires of the kingedome or the speciall propositions of his Matie and therein but to deliberat and consult, not to conclude, wch onlie does facilitat his Ma^{ts}. resolutions, & ease him in the consideracon, leaving the end still to himself; and in this can it be thought there is any diminucon or derogation to regalitie?

It was held an incomparable wisedome in H : 3 : when after many agitacōns & turnes of State wherein he had involved himselfe by other waies, that he at last applied himselfe to ye Parliam^t, and made that his Councellor; and therein he lost neither authoritie, nor reputacon, for both his estate & dignitie were before ingaged to such low condiciōns, as I feare to speake of, and by this he, not onlie recovered that againe, but gain'd somuch vpon the affections of his people, and in the opinion of others: as there was nothing wanting to him either with Strangers or at home of what hee could desire in the harts of his subiects he had soe much as they voluntarilie offered more then he did need : in the account of others he was after held soe singuler, as his goverment was a patterne. What he refered to the Parliament was not lost to himselfe; but all the wisedome and iudgment exprest then became meerely his: Our whole storie seemes but a continued instance of this by the Acts of Parliament ever expressing the wisedome and excellencies of our Kinges, for whose soever be the labour, the honor still reflects on them, & the reputation onlie beares their names.

And the advantages otherwise wch the Kinges of this land have receaved by Parliaments, are such as they should not be forgotton: for, besides ye infinite subventions and contributions graunted here, the fines and mulcts imposed vpon greate officers and delinquents (I am sorry I should bring these two soe neere to geither) theire fines I say, y^t haue beene questioned in this place haue often enlarged the treasures of our Kings, and it was a practise much vsed in former times, when officers and greate men were swolne wth corruption, to have them purged in parliament, that they hate and envie: might be taken from the Prince, and yet hee receive the benefitt of theire punishment; and the subiects haue beene soe much affected to see these spunges of the Common Wealth squeizd into the Kings cofers, that as it were in congratulation they have offered for themselves when nothing hath beene wanting; and this my thinkes should indeare the creditt of our Parliaments that they intrench not vpon, but extend the power and hono^r of the Soweraigne.

The Parliament is but the representative bodie of the kingdome, by contraction drawne into this center, like the sunne taken through a glasse, to enforce the strength and heate of his reflection, and to this forme and station it is not of it self it is thus mov'd & occasioned : *Corpus iacet inerte & cessaturum si nemo moveat,* say the Philosophers, the bodie is dull and vnapt when it hath not a spirit to move it ; is not this spirit in the hart [of] the King that hath called vs hither ? are not his graces the Beames wch through his perspective the Parliament, are to be derived to the life and benefitt of his subiects. how then can it be imagined wee should attempt against him by whome wee are ? the reason of Simpathie and participacõn aswell in pollicie as nature houlds inviolable, and what preiudice, or iniurie the King shall suffer wee must feele : he is to vs as wee are to the countrie, our verie selfe ; he is in the representive part, our principall part by the iudgment of all antient and modern Philosophers ; for the controversie hath onlie beene betweene the head and hart, and he is both. he is *vinculum per quod resp. cohæret,* (as Seneca calls him) *et spiritus vitalis quem hæc tot millia trahunt.* he is in the metaphor the breath of our nostrills, & the bond by wch wee are tied one to another : then can it not be wee should attempt against, or in any thing neglect the hono^r of him, whoe is soe much our owne ; & the mistakes that have beene this waie heertofore I beleeve have beene grounded more vpon misreport then the deserts of any from those states, whoe I know make it their speciall propositions by all their labours and indeauours to exalt and magnifie the Kinge, in whome consists the glorie and hono^r of the kingdome. it is that spotted fame that casts those ielosies, & that often through the vntimelie deliverie or report, of those things

T

wch are here conceived, before they are brought foorth, for in the dispute all things are doubtfull and vncertaine wch in the resolution conclude happilie and well. and being soe taken before theire times, they may easilie fall into misprision and soe cause theire authors to be suspected. and thus I feare some have beene heretofore traduct, whose meanings were as farr from danger as outward happiness hath beene since from them. I speake it not in pittie of theire sufferings if they have deserved it; but in sorrowe for this place that had not creditt enough to iudge oft it selfe.

To prevent those inconveniences should be now our labour, that wee be not broken or interrupted in the success of o^r indeavours. & for the first, our owne private ielosies, & destractions, as the fault seemes to be meerlie in our selves soe must the remedy, wch may be done by some generall tie or obligaĉon here of truth, and secrecie amongst o^r selues, that in noe counsell else is wanting; but in this ffor the latter, the cure is in the Kinge, & that might be as easilie effected, if either his Matie would reiect the Whispers of our enemies, or not beleeve them: for t'is those that feare o^r Parliaments that traduce them, & in the report deforme the priviledges of this place according to theire owne intentions. of himselfe his Matie cannot misconceive vs, he is wise *et omnis sapiens est bonus*, as saies the master of wisedome, therefore I haue noe doubt, but of himself his Matie will allowe vs all the priviledges, and liberties that may advance our counsells; and to this end I could wish that wee might now speciallie peticôn him, and wth some remonstrance in this point, humblie desire the continuation of those favors that our ancestors haue inioyed, wch I doubt not when his Matie shall truelie weigh vs and our loyalties, and compare vs wth the former times, but he wilbe pleased to grant : wch as it will begett confidence soe will it add diligence to our indeavours, both for the generall good, and his Ma^ts most perticuler satisfaçõn, w^thout which the same hasards follow vs that before have beene to others, and our assurance is soe little, that after much travell and time it may be said of vs, as it was of the sailor, whoe being taken from his harbour and wth contrarie windes and seas much tost in a longe storme, was inforced to putt back againe, *non multum ille navigavit, sed multum iactatus est.* the trouble, and daunger is like to be more then the profitt of the iorney."

Our next Speech—in the same Session—is extremely noticeable, though it related merely to a private bill. "A suit," the Biographer informs us, "called 'Duncombe's case,' had caused great excitement in the courts. The law of England appeared to have settled that the rights of a son born in wedlock, though the mother was so living at the time that the husband could not for a period of more than two years have had access to her, were indefeasible; and a bill had been introduced for disinherision of this supposed but spurious son. Eliot supported it with his utmost warmth and vivacity of manner" (*ibid.* p. 151). This Speech follows next in the Port Eliot volume; but as Forster has printed it, I refer the reader to vol. i., pp.

151-3. Similarly with the next Speech on the case of the Lord Treasurer Middlesex; it will be found (substantially) in vol. i., pp. 162-4.

Following these Speeches of his own, are two by the BISHOP OF LINCOLN (Williams), and one by SIR THOMAS CREWE. It is of singular interest to compare these 'reports,' made in Sir John Eliot's own hand, with the summary and notices introduced into *Negotium Posterorum*. They prove with what conscientious painstaking he sought to get at authentic materials for his great book. This holds equally of the 'precedents' and facts of all his Speeches. It is touching and impressive to discover evidence upon evidence that before he delivered his opinion or judgment he spared no cost to know at once fact and law. There is a *plethora* of extracts from all manner of recondite sources; and on these he based his arguments and appeals and counsels. It is not, therefore, to be wondered at, that feeling the solid rock beneath him, he stood immovable as that rock itself when he had come to a deliberate decision.

One very important Speech by Eliot in the Parliament at Oxford, 'August, 1625,' does not appear in *Negotium Posterorum*. It must here find a place *in extenso*. In the MS. it is carefully written by a third hand, but is shown by the marginal notes to have been read and revised throughout by himself.

Fol. 19-24.
A speech in

" Mr Speaker.

Althoughe the constant wisedome of this house of

Commons did well and worthily appeare in censureinge that ill aduised Member the last day for trenchinge soe farr into their auncient liberties; And might incourage each worthie servant of the publique here to offer freely vpp his councell and opinion. Yet since these walles cannot conceale from the eares of capcious guilty and revengfull men without, the councell and debates within, I will indeuor as my cleare minde is free from any personall distaste of any one, foe to oppose the honest thoughtes of my hart, and dischardge the best care of my trust; As noe person shall iustly taxe my innocent and publique minde, except his conscience shall make him guilty of such crimes, as worthily haue in Parliament impeached others in elder times: I will therefore wth as much of brevity as I can, sett downe howe those disorders haue by degrees sprunge vpp in o^r owne Memories. How the wisedome of the best and wisest Ages did of old redresse the like. And lastly what modest and dutifull way I would wishe to be followed by our selues in this soe happie springe of o^r hopefull Master. ffor Mr Speaker wee are not to iudge, but to present, the redresse is aboue *Ad Querimoniam vulgi.* Now Mr Speaker soe longe as those attended about our Sou^raigne Master nowe with God as had serued the late Queene of happie memorie, Debtes of the Crowne were not soe greate, Coīnissions and Grantes not soe oft complayned of in Parliament, Trade florished, Pentions not soe many though more then in the late Queenes time (ffor they exceeded not 18,000^lbs. now more then sixscore thousand poundes.) All thinges of moment carried by publique

Parliament die Augusti 1625. An°. pri°. Caroli Regis./

Nouæ Ordina: An°. 5 Ed: 2: in vita Regis.

debate at the Councell table. Noe Hono^{rs}: sett to sale or places of judicature, lawes against Priestes and Recusantes unexecuted, Resorte of Papists to Ambassadors houses barred and punished. His Matie both by dayly direction to all his ministers, and by his owne Penn declaringe his dislike of that Profession. Noe waste expences in fruitles Ambassadges. Nor any transcendent power in any one minister for matters of state. The Councell Table holdinge vpp ye fitt and aunciant dignity.

Soe longe as my Lord of Somersett stood in state of Grace, And had by his Ma^{te} fauo^r, the Trust both of the Signett and Privie Seale, he oft would glory iustly, there passed neither to himselfe or his freindes any large Grantes of his highnes lands or Pentions, ffor that wch himselfe had, he paide 20,000^{ti}. towards the Mariadge Portion of the Kings Daughter; His care was to passe noe Monopoly or illegall Grant, as some members in this House cann wittnes by his chardge vnto them, Nor giueinge way to the sale of hono^{rs}. as a breache vppon the Nobility; for such was his owne words, refuseinge Sr John Ropers Offise (then tendred to procure him to be made a Baron). The Matche wth Spaine then offered. and wth condicōn to require noe further Tolleracōn in Religion then Ambassadors are here allowed, discou^ringe theire doble dealeinge and the dangers, He diswaded his Matie from And left him soe farr in distrust of the faithe of that Kinge and his Instrument Gundomar then here resideinge, that his Matie did terme him longe time after a Juglinge Jacke: Thus stood the effect of his power wth his Matie when the clouds of his misfortunes fell vppon him.

Propositions of the Sp: King by Gundamar 1615.

What the future Aduices leadd in wee may well remember, The Treaty of Mariadge w[th] Spaine was againe renewed, Gondomar declared an honest man. Popery hartened by the admission of those vnhard of before condicōns of conniuancy. The `forces of his Ma[tie] in the Pallatinat w[th]drawne vpon Spanishe faith improued here and beleeued, by w[ch] his highnes children haue lost theire Patrimony And more money spent in fruitles Ambassadges then would haue mainteined an Army fitt to haue recouered that Countrey. Our old and fast Allies dishartened by that tedious and dangerous Treaty, And the Kinge our now master exposed to soe great a perill as noe wise and faithfull Councell would euer haue aduised. Erro[rs] in gouermen[t] lye more in misfortune by weake Councells then in Princes free actions. Artic: betweene y[e] K: and Spayne by Hinezoza.

Princes of Germany.

Itin. Caroli Principis in Hispaniam.

The losse of the County of Pontiff in ffraunce was layde to Bishopp Wickhams Chardge in the first of Rich : the Second for perswaideinge the King to forbeare sendinge ayde when it was required. Rot. Parl. A°.i°. Rici 2. Gascoyn. Lincol. libr.

The losse of the Duchie of Mayn a capitall crime in Parliament layde to De la Poole : 28. H. 6. in single and vnwisely treateinge of a Marriadge in ffraunce. A Spanish Treaty lost the Palatinat. Rot. Parl. 28 H. 6. Gascoign. in Bibliothec. Lincoln. Oxonn Anioy. Mayn.

What Councell hath procured soe great power to the Spanish Agent neuer before, to effect freedome to soe many Preests as hath byn of late, and to become a Sollicito[r] almost in euery Tribunall, for the ill affectted Subiect[s] of the State, is worthe Inquirie.

What Graunts of Imposicōns before crossed haue lately byn complayned of in Parliament, as that of Alehouses, Parl. A°. Jacobi Regis.

Gouldthridde, pretermitted Custome and many more. The least of wch would haue byn 30mo. Edri: 3. adiudged in Parliament a heynous Crime, as well as those of Lions and Latimer.

<small>Rot. Parl. A°. 30 Edri. 3.</small>

The Duke of Suffolke in Henry the 6. time, for procuringe such and other Grant^s in derogaĉon of the Comon Lawe, was iudged by Parliament. The guift of Honors, kept as the most sacred Treasure of the State, now sett to sale.

<small>Rot. Parlia: A°. 28 H. 6. in Art. contra Ducem Suff.</small>

Parliaments haue byn Suito^{rs} to the Kinge to bestowe those Graces as in the times of Ed: 3. Hen: 4. and Hen: the. 6. more nowe leadd in by that waie only then all the merritts of ye best deservours haue gott this last 500 yeares, soe tender was the care of elder times, that it is an Article 28 of Hen. 6. in Parliament against De la Poole Duke of Suffolke, that he had procured for himselfe and some fewe others, such Titles of Hono^r And thos soe irreguler that he was the first that euer was Earle Marquis and Duke of one, and the self same Place.

<small>Parl. A°. Ed. 3.</small>
<small>Parl. A°. Hen. 4.</small>
<small>Rot. Parl. A°. 28°. H. 6.</small>
<small>Par. A°. Hen. 6.</small>

Edward the first restrained the nomber in Policy that would haue challenged a right by Tenure. And how this disproporĉon may suite wth profitt to the State, wee cannot tell: Great Desert^s haue now noe other Recompence then costly Reward^s from the Kinge, for we now are taught the vild Price of that wch was once inestimable.

<small>Claus. A°. 23 Ed. primi.</small>

If worthie persons haue byn advanced frely to places of greatest Trust I shalbe gladd. Spencer was condempned in the 15 Ed. 2. for displaceinge good servants about the Kinge, and puttinge in his freinds and followers. Not

<small>Parl. A°. 25 Ed. 2.</small>

leaveinge way either in the Church or Comonwealth to any before a fine was paide to him or his dependant℮.

The like in parte was layd by Parliament on De la Poole. Parl. a°. 28. H: 6.

It cannot be but a sadd heareinge vnto vs all what my Lo: Treasurer the last day told vs, his Ma^ts great Debts, highe Ingagem^ts and presente wantes, the noice whereof I wishe may euer rest inclosed W^th in thes walles, for what of Incouragem^t it may be to our enemies and of disharteninge to our freinds, I cannot tell. The daunger of thes if any that haue bin the Cause is greate and fearefull.

It was noe small motiue to Parliam^t of H: 3 to banishe the King's halfe Brothers for pcuringe to themselues soe lardge proportion of the Crowne lands to the Kinges want. Clausa°. 44: H: 3 regist. st alb:

Gaueston & Spencer for doeinge the like for themselues & followers in Ed: 2. time, both exiled. And the Lady Vesey for procuringe the like for her Brother Beaumont were banished the Court. Parl. a°; 3: Ed: 2. Parl: a°: 15 Ed. 2. Noue ord: a°. 5: Ed: 2.

Michael de la Poole was condempned: 10. Rich: 2. in Parliam^t. amongst other Crimes for procuringe landes & Pentions from the Kinge, And turneinge the Subsidies to other endes then the Grant intended.

His Grandchild William Duke of Suffolke for ye like vnderwent the like censure: 28: H. 6. Parl: a°: 28: H. 6.

The greate Bishopp of Winchester Wickham 50: Ed: the 3. was put vppon the Kinges mercy by Parliament for wasteinge in time of peace the Revenues of the Crowne and guifts of the people to the yearely oppression of the Comonwealth. Parl: 2°: 50: Ed. 3.

Ex Articl: contra Ducem Somers: A°. 3. Ed. 6.	Offences of this nature were vrged to the ruininge of the last Duke of Somersett in Ed : the 6th: time ; More fearefull Examples may be found to[o] frequent in Recorde.
Cronicon s^t. Albani.	Such Improvidence and ill Councell leadd He : 3 into soe greate a straite as after he had pawned some pts of his
Gul. Gisborne Math: Paris. Histo: Rams: monaster: Rot. claus. 26. H. 3. Hist: feria Conses.	foraigne Teritories, broke vpp his house, And sought his diett at Abbies and Religious houses, ingaged not only his owne Jewells, but thos of the shrine of St Edward at Westm^r. was in the ende notwthstanding constrayned to lay to pawne as some of his Successo^{rs} after ded vppon the Like improvidence *Magnā Coronā Angliæ* the Crowne of England.
Ex libro originali in coll: Lincoln Oxonii.	To drawe yo^u out to life the Image of a former Kingℓ extremities, I will tell yo^u what I found since this Assembly at Oxforde written by a reverend man Twice Chauncello^r of this Place : his name was Gascoyne, a man that sawe the Tragedy of De la Poole : he tells yo^u that the Reuenues of the Crowne were soe rent away by ill Councell, that the Kinge was inforced to liue *De Taliis et quindenis populi*, That the Kinge was growne in debt *Quinquies Centena milia libras*, That his greate fauorite in treateinge a foraigne Marriadge had lost his Master a foraigne Duchie, That to worke his ends he had caused the Kinge to adiorne the Parliament *In villis et remotis partibus regni :* where *Propter defectum hospitii et victualium* fewe should attende ; And by shiftinge that Assembly from place to place to inforce, I will vse the Authors words, *illos paucos qui remanebant de cōmunitate regni concedere Regi quamuis pessima*. And when the Parliament

endeuoured by any Act of Resumption the iust and frequent way to repaire the languisheinge estate of the Crowne (for all frō Hen: 3: but one vntill the sixt yeare of Hen: the 8th: haue vsed it). This greate man tould the Kinge it was *ad dedecus Regis,* and forced him from it, At which the Comons answered Although *vexata laboribus et expensis quod nunquam concederent taxam Regi.* vntill by authoritie of Parliament: *resumeret actualiter omnia pertinentia Coronæ Angliæ :* And that it was *maius ad dedecus Regis* to leaue soe many poore men in intollerable want, to whome ye Kinge stood then indebted, Yet nought could all good Councell worke vntill by Parliam^t. that badd great man was banished, wch noe sooner done, An Acte of Resumption followed the Inrolement of the Act of his Exilement. Parl: 28: H: 6.

It was a speedinge Article against the Bishopp of Winchester and his Brother in the time of H: the 3. that they had ingrossed the person of the Kinge from his other Lords : it was not forgotten against Gaueston and Spencer in Ed: 2: time. Claus 44 H. 3. Registr Rams: 4to. Parl: 3°: et 5°: Ed: 2.

The vnhappie Ministers of Rich: 2. H: 6. and the last Ed: felt the weight to their Ruyne: the like Erro^{rs} I hope wee shall not complaine in Parliament againe of such. Parl: 23: Rich: 2. Parl: 28: Hen: 6.

I am glad we haue neither iust Cause or vndutifull disposicōns to appoint the Kinge a Councell to redresse those Erro^{rs} by Parliament as those of 42. H: 3. Wee doe not desire, as 5. H: 4. or 29: H. 6 the remoueinge from about the Kinge of evill Councellors. Art. contra Soms^t. 3 Ed. 6. Claus. 42. H: 3. Parl: 5 Hen: 4. Parl: 28: Hen: 6.

Wee doe not request a choice by name as 14: Ed: 3: Parl: 14: Ed. 3.

148   SUPPLEMENT.

Parl: 3. 5. 11.   3: 5: 11. of Rich: the: 2: 8. H: 4 or 31. H: 6 : Nor to
Rich. 2.
Parl: 8: H: 4.   swere thē in Parliam⁺ as: 35 : of Ed: the first : 9: Ed: 2:
Parl: 31. H: 6.   or 5. Rich: 2: Or to lyne them out theire directions of
Parl: 35: Ed:
primi.   Rule as 43: H: 3. and 8. of H: 6:
Parl: 9: Ed: 2.
Parl: 5: Rich: 2   Or desire that wch H: 3. did promise in his 42 yeare,
Claus 43: Hen: *Se acturum omnia per assensum Magnatum de Concilio*
3.
Parl: 8: H: 6.   *suo electo et sine eor̄ assensu nihil:* Wee only in loyall
Claus 42 H: 3.   duty offer vpp our humble desires that since his Matie
hath wth aduised Judgement elected soe wise religious
and worthie seruantes to attend him in that highe Im-
ployment, He wilbe pleased to aduise wth them to-
geither a way of Remedy for those disasters in State,
leadd in by longe security and happie Peace And not w^th
younge and single Councell. The Successe hereof wee
neede not doubt when wee looke backe to the euer
readines of his sacred Matie to give vs our desires. And his
noble Constancy euer to make good his neuer violated
worde vnto vs, vnles by our refusall nowe of some
moderate some to assist his Matie. in this his first and I
hope succesfull Action, wee open him the vntroden way,
as yet of harshe deniall.

                    Oxoniæ in Parliamento
                        die Augusti."

Equally important with this, is a Speech on 'Supply'
penned wholly in Sir John Eliot's own handwriting, as
follows :—

Fol. 25-27.   "I have observed in ye passages of this day ye divers motions that have beene made & y° excellencie of their intendm⁽ˢ⁾. I have cald to mind yᵉ proceedings heer of former times. I have remembered the affections & indeavʳˢ. of oʳ predecessʳˢ, I have wᵗʰ myself revolv'd (& wᵗ. in soe short a time occasionally I must doe), cast vp̄ wᵗ. successes wᵗ issues they have had, & from thenc drawne, a consideration to oʳ selves what we may now expect, wᵗ course we may best hould, for from thenc ther may be a coniecture made vnto oʳ p̄sent hopes, the effect & consequence of all acts being impli'd in yᵉ iudgmᵗ of their entranc & prosecution, wherin yᵉ latter times I doubt have faild either through p̄cipitation & to[o] much hast or by impatience & importunitie preventing their owne desires in the to[o] affectionat & ernest desire of them, as it's noted of yᵉ Samians in yᵉ like case for p̄ssing vpon Meander *cui iustissimo vivorum volenti esse non licuit*, as saith that storie, they vrgd their suit soe violently vpon him as they gave him not time to answear or grant it, being willing. In all things time & order are of best advantage, the one the measure the other the weight of all proceedings, & the greatest pʳiudice or hindrance in business that can happen comes by anticipation or disorder, for if ther be not time nothing can be done : wᵗʰout order & direction ther can be made noe vse of time, & this I beleeve we have heertofore seene verified in our selvs (whither by act soe contriv'd or incidentally followīg our owne oversights I will not iudge) but the effects doe shew it yᵗ we sufferd, sufferd in the last, sufferd in yᵉ form̄ parliam⁽ˢ⁾. I will not enumerat all oʳ sufferings that way but make an intimation for yʳ memories how they times have slipt vs, how they overpast vs, before we could conclude, nay beefore we could almost begin the business we came for. The business we came for did I say ? noe ; I am then mistaken, that we dispatch't betimes, if not to[o] soone, the business it is we should come for I mean, y⁶ countries business, y⁶ publicke care, y⁶ common good, y⁶ generall affairs of K. & Kᵐ, not y⁶ satisfaction of anie privat ends or hopes : these have overslip't vs, these have past beside vs, though not wᵗʰout mention yet wᵗʰout effect.

How these things have beene governed & directed I will not now beginn a search or scrutinie but wᵗʰ what modestie I may wᵗʰout dishonor to soe great a Counsell assume the occasion to oʳ selves, oure owne facilities, oʳ owne credulityes that deceavd vs, & from them I wilbe build [:bold] to derive some observations for the future, for y⁶ time we are now in, how we may sort it, how we may manage it to oʳ best advantage & the common good. And first, I will make one generall proposition wᶜʰ I shall afterwards reduce into some particulers, & that is for supplie, supplie I mean for the Country, supplie in governmᵗ., supplie in iustice, supplie in reformation, supplie in aid of oʳ long neglected greivances. that these things may beginn oʳ labors, that we may settle them, that we prepare it, that we present it, naie I will goe farther, that we attend & take our answears before we admitt in other things either treatie or debate. But me thinks I hear some Courtier saying to me yᵘ goe now to[o] farr, yᵘ exceed yʳ limitts, its not a parliamentarie course yᵘ propose, yᵘ have noe p̃sident for it ; I crave him pardon yᵗ speaks or thinks it ; if I err 'tis out of love not out of flattery, & though I am not warranted, yet I am induc't by former practises, if changing the persons doe not change the case. Did we not the last parliam^t. freelie give y^t session to the King vpon the promise, & assurance of his word to have ye next for vs ? did we not in the parl. before doe the like, & in both exprest asmuch faith & love, as could be expected from poore sub^{ts} ? did we not in 18 of King Jam[es] grant two subsidies wch were presently confirmed & past wthout a Session ? have we not of o^r parts ended wth trust enough these times to endear the creditt of o^r Soveraigne ? may we not iustly challeng it as meritt now in y^t respect to have his Matie. beginn wth vs ? or is it not the same in reason as fit vs to beginn wth him ? Surelie it is ; the business is the same, & though ther were noe law of retaliation, this would perswade & move it that w^t is the Countries is ye King's good, for those that will distinguishe or divide them, I dare be bould to saie are neither good schollers, nor good statesmen. We then have broken presidents for the K. let it not seeme strange we should now desire ye K. may doe the like for vs : let vs receave some fruite of all o^r confidenc and hope, that we may send it as a satisfaction to o^r countries, & as I know twill affect y^m, it shall harten me to straine my self heerafter wholy into the King's desires, this being granted now; wch generall I shall therfore desire y^u to take into y^r memory & considerations, as that wch may prepare, naie that wch must assure our passage to the rest.

and that according to this we may the better husband o^r times, & business, I will heere descend into some perticulers

SUPPLEMENT.

W^{ch} I conceave next fit for y^r resolutions, wherin part I will take from that that has past now, part from ye memorie of o^r last consultations, part I will add as it shalbe necessary, in all submittinge to y^r greater iudgm^{ts} either to be altered or reformed. And first I will propose the consideration of the King's estate, as that wch is most necessary, equallie necessary both for him & vs; necessary in point of honor, necessary in point of saftie, that ther may be a sufficient means to comport the State, and dignitie of soe great a Matie & to supplie him on all occasions wth power & strength to amate & check his enemyes, & to protect his frinds. Y^u know in this how much we have sufferd for the late times, through whose occasion I speake not, what p̃iudice we have had, what losses we have sustained, losses abroad, losses at home, losses to o^r frinds, losses to o^r selves, how ye King's treasures have been exhausted, how his revenewes are impaird, how his reputation's lessened : in w^t strait o^r most gratious Soveraigne was left to his estate, who has power to speake it, who has hart to thinke it wthout an in ward bleeding of his sowle for soe much wrong of Matie. soe long time vnpunishd ? *thesaurus regius anima reip:* ye treasure of ye K. is ye life of ye sub^t. hurt y^t y^u wound ye K^m. cutt of ye King's revenews y^u cutt of ye principall means of y^r owne safties, & not onlie disable him to defend y^u but enforce that wch y^u conceave [an] offenc, ye extraordinary resort to his sub^{ts} for supplies, & the more then ordinary waies of raising them. This in form̃ times has not beene thought a consideration vnworthie of the parls. neither have our Kings taken it to be dishonorable to remitt that care to them, but as their easiest, & safest waies have wth the labors of ye parls. fill'd their owne coffers, wch how it has beene practis'd heer, how it has been vsd in other parts, what resumptions of lands, w^t accounts of officers, what infinit restitutions have beene by that means made to the Crownes, when it shalbe needfull vpon the more perticular debate heerof I shalbe bould to tell y^u, & what I may conceave fitt for redresse, & remedy.

in ye second place, I will propose ye account of o^r subsidies & fifteenths granted 21°. wch I conceave soe necessary to be exactly taken, as we suffer much already for ye honor & wisdome of this place, & in ye generall misfortunes that have happend that it has beene soe long delaid : I confesse ther was an entraie made to it heer last parl. a shew of prosecution continued at Oxford, some mention of ye accountants but wthout effect; some generall answears were taken, as of ye treasurer & part of ye counsell of warr, but for ye rest & the perticulers they were not prest but left as things forgotten. What is this but to make a parl: ridiculous, to p̃tend integritie & zeale for ye Common Cause & to desert it, to draw ye iudgm^{ts} of ye howse into noe regard: consists the virtue only in shew or words? is it a discharge of o^r duties in this place to seeme affectionat, & carefull not to be soe? doe these walls comprehend o^r duties, & must they not extend wth out them? pardon me I beseech y^u pardon me in speaking freely, I shall as freelie doe the service y^u command me: it stands not wth our honor, it stands not wth our gravities in this place to be noted careless or vncertaine, & I beseech yᵘ once againe it may not seeme in this.

yᵉ reasons at this time for pressing this account are more then ordinarie, & the weight & greatness of it I beleeve is much mistaken, for to me its noe small fear that the former omissions have occasiond much of that p̃iudice in our affaires that has happend since ; & the extent & reach of yᵉ accᵒ now, I take to be soe large as it involves the consideration of oʳ last adventure, & the search of the causes of our vnhappiness therin : for as I vnderstand it both from yᵉ memorie of our intentions in passing the act wᵗʰ such conditions & from yᵉ word & letter of yᵉ act it self not only the monies, but the service in wᶜʰ it is imploid should be accompted for, & therin not the Trer̃s & Coun: of Warr alone but all others who by office or command should be interest therin were to be examined of ther carriage doeings & proceedings & to receave such iudgmᵗˢ from yᵉ parl. as their cause meritts, & now I beseech yᵘ cast yʳ eyes about, veiw the state we are in, consider yᵉ losses we have receaved, weigh the wreckt & ruind honor of oʳ nation (or yᵉ incomparable hopes of oʳ most excellent Soveraigne checkt' in their first designe) search the preparation, examine yᵉ goeing foorth, let yʳ wisdomes travell through the whole action, to know yᵉ faultie, to discerne yᵉ fault, & I p̃sume, though no man vndertake it you'le finde yᵉ antient Genius of this kingdome will rise vp to be an accuser. is this a light & easie matter of accᵗ ? is yᵉ reputation & glorie of oʳ nation of a small valew ? are yᵉ walls & bulwarks of oʳ Kᵐ. of no esteeme ? were yᵉ numberless lives of o^r lost men not to be regarded? I know it cannot soe harbour in an Englishe thought: our honor is ruin'd, our ships are suncke, our men perisht, not by ye sword, not by an enemy, not by chance, but apparantly discernd before-hand out of strong p̃dictiõns, by those we trust, by that p̃tended care & thrift that vshers all our misfortunes. I could lose my self in this complaint, ye miseries, ye calamities wch o^r western parts have both seene & fealt, strike soe strong an apprehension on me. but ye perticulers are to manie to be instanct now: in their times y^t will appear quite fully as incidents to that acc^o, wch if we therfore slight or overcast, maie then our sufferings evermore correct vs.

but perchance it wilbe said this concerns vs not, our monie was long since spent in other actions, nothing remaynd to this: to prevent the obiection I will make this answear, I know nothing soe prosperous or good in those former actions that may extenuate much less excuse the faults of this, & this I am sure falls wthin ye compass of those ends to wch our money was given, for besides ye generall of Warr, in wch it is included, it's in point containd in ye fowrth perticuler, ye setting forth of ye Navie, naie it is the verie perticuler it self that was intended, & I am sure our monie advanc^t, if not concluded this preparation wch makes it a proper sub^t of ye acc^o. & I hope in conclusion will make it profitable, both for his Matie & vs.

vpon these perticulers therfore I will contract my motion, this of ye acc^o, that of ye Kings estate, wherin I shall desire ther may be a settled order for their handling, daies prefix't to take them into consideration, Committees therto specially appointed, from wch nothing may divert them, that by such seasonable & timelie beginning we may have a happie period & conclusion, & by such order preserve our times free from interruption, & produce, something worthy the expectation of the Countrie & our owne labors; and the generall [   ] wch I at first proposd I would not have forgotten, that vntill these be perfitted & such other matters as shalbe necessary for the supplie of the Countrie, noe mentions, noe overtures, noe motions for others to be taken, but that the common cause may have a full precedence, wch out of our affectionat & pious care, to secure ye waies in wch we are to walke, to prevent those preventions vnder wch we have heertofore soe much sufferd, to preserve the mutuall honor & interests of my prince, & countrie, I most humbly move."

A second speech on 'Supply' in the same session, made on Rudyard's motion on the King's inauguration-day, is again in a third hand, but has corrections, interlineations, and further additions by Eliot. Here it is:—

Fol. 28-33
2 Carol. reg. noted by Sr B. R, to be the Kings birthday.

Vpon the Proposition for Supply.

"This daye was begunne wth a happie auspice, and I hope wee shall giue itt as happie a conclusion, though our debates may be wth some varietie of opinions, yett I doubt nott but our resolucõns wilbe one, and what difference soever ther may be in pticulars, we shall concurr wholie in the generall for the good of the Kinge and Kingdome, & to that direct oʳ motions as to their Center, where we shall fix in oʳ periods and rest. the gent. that àt first wᵗʰ the advantage of the tyme, did induce this pʳposition for supplie made a fine insinuation by discourse of the state and affaires of Christendom, inferringe from thence out of their relacõn to vs the dangers wee are in, and soe pressinge the necessitie of our ayde, that therby the Kinge might be enabled to resist them, wherein (as his ptestacõn was that the feares wᶜʰ he p̃tended were not pañicke,) I shall add this to in horror of that gentelman yᵗ I hope they are not pañicke as artifices to move vs from the fixt station of our reasons; but wᵗʰ satisfaction vnto him and the whole world besides, we shall soe observe & note them, as things worthy consideracõn & respect, yett not of such necessitie & hast, as should decline the gravitie of parliamᵗ & the due course of our proceedings: but yᵗ. wee may therein still reteyne the preservation of our orders, & exampled dignitie and wisedome of our Ancestoʳˢ.

A speciall respect in this proposition that is made, must be to the abilitie of the subᵗᵉ, what power he has to answere the occasions of the K: for I remember a storie of Themistocles that when for the service of the Athenians he required certeyne monies of the Andrians whoe were then tributaries to that state, he was answered that they were denied to furnish him by the two great Goddesses of their Countrie povertye and impossibilitie that then sweyd them, & such powers haue noe resistance; and if there should be the like diuinities wth vs, certainlye our excuse were as lawfull if we now refuse as they did. but to know this we must first looke vppon the condition of the kingdome & the state: that being knowne in truthe, & compard wth the occasions that are extant, will best give a direction to our iudgments: therfore wth this we will beginne, wch must shew vs, through that perspective the power & abilitie we are in, wch can only crowne our purposes what ever wee intend, & wth out wch all the p̃mises wee make wilbe of none effect. This wee may consider in two p̱ticulars of estate of will, (for though the latter be not properlie an abilitie but a disposic̃ōn), yet because its that wch must give motion to the other, I shall soe call it here & therein give yo^{u} some fewe observac̃ōns out of the reasons of these times, and from the examples of the Elder. for the first the abilitie of estate, I will not speake much singlie by it selfe but as it shall happen by mixture wth the other, for though manye things might be urged vppon the p̃sent condic̃ōn of the sub^{te} of dilation to this pointe, yet I am confident their shall neuer want abilitie in England and Englishmen, to supplie their Kinge wth aydes necessarye or fitt for the advantage and suppo^{rt}. of all his iust occasions. In that of will then, how the people stand dispos'd, how they are affected ther are many things observable for o^{r} affayres abroad, for our affayres att home, abroad in our late expedic̃ōn vnto Cales. what encouragment, what hart, what affection can it giue to that, that is required ? the oppressions, the corruptions, the exactions, the extorsions are soe infinite as almost noe pte is free, naie hardlie a man but has some cause drawen from those abuses wch doth both disharten and disable him, honors made marchantable, iudiciall places sold, & yet the rule acknowledged *venders* [*venderis*] *quæ emeris gentiũ ius esse.* Cicero in one of his orations against Verres tells a storie how the pvinces on a tyme were petition^{rs} to the Senate that the lawe *de pecuniis repetundis* might be repealed againe, by wch. all the corruptions of their officers were made punishable. the Senate (as he observes it) when they saw the scope of their petition begann to wonder att the thing and desir'd to know the reason whye the repeale was sought of that wch was onlie in favour of themselues, but when they heard their answere they were satisfied that though twas true the law was soe intended yett the successe was otherwise, and whereas before their officers not feareinge to be questioned made their exaccõns simplie for themselues and for the satisfaccõn of their owne & private families and fortunes, now beinge held in terro^r by this lawe they were enforct to make them frends at Court to pcure them advocates, to procure them patrons for defence, if their cause should come in questiond. naie to corrupt the Judges soe as they that before made onlye single exactions for themselues, now did double their oppressions to that height that the spoile of the pvinces seemed to be devided amongst many, which likewise multiplie the iniuries wth the occasions, & by that gaue them y^t reason of complainte. what applicacõn might this now haue to vs? how does this sorte wth the experience of these tymes? were not the truth and dignitie of that author w{th}out question, it might bee taken rather for a prophisey of ours, then for a storye of that age: the discription is soe like to the practises wth vs, that it seemes to be a meere Character of our sufferings: its too visible what oppressions haue been made, not onlye oppressions of the subiecte but oppressions on the Kinge, his Treasures are exhausted, his revenewes are consumed, aswell as the Treasures and faculties of the sub{te}. wherein many handes are excersised, diuers haue their gleanings but the harvest and great gatheringe comes to one, who must ptect the rest and for his countenance drawes all others to him as his Tributaries whoe are enforc't by that not only to pillage for themselues, but him, and to the pportion of his avarice and ambicōn wch makes the abuse, & iniurie the greater. this cannot but disharten, this cannot but discourage all men well affected, all men well dispos'd to the advancment and happines of the K : and w{th}out some reformacōn in these things I know not what willes or what abilities men cann haue to giue a new supplie; yett that it may not be mistaken if ther should be an insistance vppon this to stope the pposition for the psent, I will vouch two denialls in like causes from the psidents of our Ancesto{rs}. in ould times wherein yett they concluded wth a grant, and though in the beginninge of the parliam{ts}, as now, for like reasons they refus'd yett in the same sittings they consented when vppon remōstrance of their burdens & necessities to the Kinge they had satisfaccōn in their greivances wch were soe like to ours, in all things but the time as I hardlie cann distinguish them. The first psident was in 16 H : 3.

when the comons beinge required to make a supplie vnto the Kinge excusd themselues, because saies the record the[y] saw all things disordered by those that were about him, but when vppon their advise he had resum'd the lands of the crowne that were vnnecessarilie giuen away, when he had giuen way to the question of his ministers and not spared that great officer of his Court H. de Burgo a favorite never to be paraleld but now haueinge been the only minion both to ye Kinge then liveinge and to his father wch was dead, when they had seenn as another author sayes those spunges of the Comonwealth squezed into the Kings coffers, though they had formerlie denied it, they then did grant an ayd & in the same sittinge wch they had refus'd, haveinge for the Kings good some satisfacc̄on in what they did desire, they at length consented, and in such measure & ꝑportion as the Kinge himselfe confest it was more then was enough. The second p̄sident was in x^mo. R. 2. wherein I shall desire yo^u to observe the likeness of some pticulars, for the placeinge and displaceinge of great officers, in wch ther was the Tre: changd twise, the Chancellor thrise and soe of others w^thin the space of two yeares, and how many shiffts, changes, and rechanges cann this kingdome now instance in like tyme to parable wth that ?, 2^ly ther had beenn monies formerlie granted & not accounted for, and yo^u know soe it is yet wth vs. 3^ly there were new aides required wth a declarac̄on of the Kings occasions and estate, and this likewise agrees wth our condition. yett then for those and other exceptions made against the E: of Suffolke de la Poole the minion of that tyme of whome they said, y^t he

Y

had misadvis'd the K : misimploy'd his Treasures, interverted his revenewes : the supplie demanded was refus'd vntill vppon the petition of the Com̃ons he was remov'd both from his offices and the Courte, and a comission likewise granted for the rectifieinge of the Kings estate, wch because it impo^{rts} an excellent intention and purpose of that pliam^t. (though it had not the successe and fruite it meritted) I will be bold breiflye to observe the heads & grounds it had, vppon wch yo^u shall make yor owne inference and Judgm^t. it beginns thus. Whereas o^r Soſſaigne Lord the Kinge pceaveth by the greivous complaints of his Lordes and Comons that his pfitts rents and revenewes of his Realme, by the singuler and insufficient Counsell and euill goũm^t. of &c̃. be soe much wthdrawen, wasted, aliened, given, granted, destroyed and evill dispended, that he is soe much impoſished and voyd of Treasure and goods, and the substance of the crowne soe much diminished that his estate may not wholye be susteyned as apperteyneth &c̃ : the Kinge of his free will at the request of the Lt: and Comons, hath ordeyned &c̃. to examine as well the estate and goũm^t. of his house as also all the rents revenewes and pfitts &c̃. and all manno^r of guifts. grantes alienations, and confirmac̃ons &c̃ of lands tenem^{ts} rents &c̃. bargained or sould to the pĩudice of him and his crowne. and of all Jewell[s] and goods wch were his grand fathers at the tyme of his death and wher the[y] be become &c̃.

If now there were a such a Comission heer wth vs to examine the revenewes of the Kinge, to veiwe that antient garden, & those sweet flowers o'th Crowne, & wher they are now become, & how the inclosure being let downe, its made a common pasture. Searching for the treasures & iewells that were lefte bye that ever blessed princes of neuer dyinge memorie Queen Eliz (o^r those iewells the pride and glorie of this kingdome wch haue made it soe farr shining beyond others, would they were heer wthin the compass of these walles to be veiwd & seene by vs, to be examined in this place, their very name and memorie transports me, (but I must recall my self to the labor of this day) if I saye such a Comission were now extant to those that faithfullie would execute itt, what advantage would it render to the K: that would remove all need to presse supplies from vs. But I must retorne to the observaçõns wch I left, this Comission beinge then granted and that fauorit removed, the pliam^t consented to the ayd, and in the same sittinge they refused it, vppon this reasonable satisfaccõn (wch tended only to the Kings good & benefit) they at last granted & accorded it and left y^t. example to posteritie, that alwayes to complie is not the dutie of a Councellor. But vppon these observations of the Elder to draw a conclusion for this tyme, w^t shall we now doe? shall wee refuse the ayd that is required, or delay it vntill there shalbe satisfaccõn given in such things as we reasonablie doe desire? noe I would not doubt the iustice of his Matie therein, but reteyne a confidence of him equall to his goodnesse, and that confidence I doubt not wilbe more p̃valent then pswasions *fidelem si putaveris, facies,* saith Seneca, that confidence of ours will make him I hope the more confident of vs, and for the concurrence easier in all matters & affaires, in the assurance of wch let vs now doe as our ffathers did before vs, present our greivances & complaints that the satisfaction given in them may prepare the affections of the people, & in the meane time soe farr yeeld to the proposition for supplie that we make a promise of the ayd wch is vrgd for by the King; but for the act, that may haue leasure to attend the dispach of the rest of our affayres, to w^h I hope this pliam^t is auspitious, as in the begining this day was pphisied to the pliam^t: from both wch I desire may be derived a full streame of happines and felicitie both to the King & Kingdome."

The memorials of the 3^d. Parliament begin with a great Speech of the Patriot on its opening, of Religion and Liberty. Here it is :—

Fol. 36-38.

" It has been well propounded for a generall overture to our worke, that the manie points of consideration in this P. are to be the matters of relig. & our lib. whose necessities require a present aid & succor, & whose safties comprehend all our happiness & hopes.

What dangers they sustaine, what fears are now vpon them, may be collected from the former apprehensions of this place, or from the present reasons of the time, in wch from new occasions, new impressions are contracted, & by addition of new causes, an addition of new fears. In rell: the countenancing & favoring of papists, the imploiment & preferm^t of their Sectaries, the allowanc & admission of their preists, the neglect & remission of the lawes, all publickly, all frequently, all confidentlie in practise: naie, & almost all their [blank in MS.] actuated, & asmuch as borrowd & subordinat greatness might effect, the trulie pious & religious discountenanc't, their preferm^{ts}. hindred, their imploiments stop't, their ministries opposd & by new lawes & inquisitions questiond & disturbd: what argum^{ts} are these? what demonstration doe these make, but of a plott & practise for the subversion of the truth?

In the lib: the invasions have beene made vpon that sacred relicke of our ancestors; the attempts vpon our goods, the attempts vpon our persons; our monies taken, our wares & marchandises seisd; loanes, benevolences, contributions, impositions levied, & exacted: our bodies hurried & imprisond, & the power & execution of the Lawes vilified and contemnd; naie (but that such actions could not pass wthout the knowledge of his Matie in whose intention lives nothing but truth & goodness, & whose virtue, I am confident, has not beene consenting to the rest, in any pointe, as to a willing violation of the lawes, but as otherwise it might be represented, & inform'd; but that such actions, I say, could not pass wthout the knowledg of his Ma^{te}: whose iustice is a sanctuarie to all his loyall sub^{ts}) I am doubtfull the attempt had yet gone further to a higher pointe of enterprise, & we had hardly kept the securitie of our lives. but that wch is more then lives, more then the lives & liberties of thousands, then all our goods, all our interests & faculties, the life, the libertie of the p. the privilidges & immunities of this h. wch are the basses & support of all the rest what preiudice has it sufferd? how has it beene attempted? how violentlie, how impetuouslie assaulted? y^u cannot but remember it, y^u cannot but observe it that it yet shakes wth the shocke it has indurd. What doe these inferr? what construction doe these make? are they not plaine argum^{ts} of danger? doe they not by induction conclude reasons of fear & ielosie? I presume in a truth soe evident & cleer, noe contradiction can be made but all mens harts confess it.

nor are these dangers single, or consisting in termes seperat & divided that in the preiudice & danger of rell: we might retaine the saftie & securitie of our lib: or (on the contrary) in the danger & preiudice of our lib: ther might be a saftie & securitie in rell: if soe, part of the fear might be extenuated, & the dangers would seeme less, wch are now somuch augmented by coniunction, & mutuall necessities betweene them, that ther cannot be a securitie in either, wthout the confederation of them both. noe s^{rs}; such are their interests, & relations, such reciprocall dependencies they have, & wth such helps & advantages to each other, that, on the other side, in opposition to the danger, this ground & position we may laie, That wthout a change & innovation in our lib: ther is noe fear of an innovation in rell: & wthout an innovation in rell: ther is no fear of change or innovation in our lib: (I speake wth submission alwayes to the divine power & providence whose secrets none can penetrat) but in probability I say from the argum^{ts} & deductions of reason, (& I hope to shew it cleerlie) That an innovation in our pollicie cannot be introduc't but by an adverse strength & partie in relligion: nor can rell: have that wound to meet soe strong a partie of hir enemies while the antient pollicie is mayntaind, that is while our lawes & liberties are in force :

the reason of the former, Nature it self presents vs, & we shall not neede more evidenc then that noe man is naturally an enemie to himself, those that are borne in libertie doe all desire to live soe; but the antiente lib : of this kingdome what comparison may they have ? the freedome of this nation, the felicities it has had in the glorie & honor of the pr : in the quiet & tranquilitie of the people ; the generall & common happiness wch soe long we have enioy'd vnder our owld lawes & liberties, who could be drawen to leave them ? what ignorance would disert them to submitt to the fears & incertainties of a change ? none ; I may bouldly say ther's none of a sound hart or iudgment, naie that wilbe guided but by sence; none, but some rotten members, men of seduc't & captiv'd vnderstandinges, who to the quailes & manna sent from heaven, prefer the flesh-potts & garlicke of the Egiptians, none but that false partie in rell, wch to their Ro. idoll will sacrifice all other inte-rests & respects : none but such as have swallowd downe that Sote the Leaven of the Jesuits, can be possest wth this ignorance or stupiditie ; soe to forgett their pr. soe to forgett their Country, soe to forgett themselves, and wthout such a fals partie of our selves, such an intestine faction wthin vs, noe forraigne power can doe vs preiudice (besides the strength & valor of our nation, in that defeat, we having nature & G. to aide vs. the frame & constitution of this state, therin answearing to the ground & center that it stands on, the Earth, wch a little winde w^thin it makes to t[r]emble but noe outward storm or violence can move; soe as (I say) but for a false partie in rell: our lib: are safe.

ffor the other part of the position that I made, that the safetie of rell: depends vpon the saftie of our liberties, the reason is apparant in the force & letter of our lawes, wch first in the generall provide against all formes of innovation; & also in perticuler take care to prevent the practise of our enemies, by exclusion of their instrum^ts, by restraining of their proselites, by abolishing their ceremonies, their sorceries; soe as while these lawes continue, while they retaine their power & operation in that pointe likewise we are safe, that ther cannot be an innovation in rell: w^thout a change likewise in the pollicie. if this truth were not perspicuous, we have examples to confirme it, wherin y^r owne experiences can help me. if y^u consult y^r memories but for the storie of these times, for a few years past, since wee first enterd into those vnhappie treaties wth the Spa: (that vniversall patron of the Cath:) since we have vsd a remission of the lawes, a lessening & extenuation of their rigor; since their sharpness, their severitie has declin'd, and their life & execution has been measur'd by that gentle Lesbian rule; how have our enemies prevaild? how infinitly have they multiplied? what an increase of poperie has' ther beene? what bouldness what confidence has' it gotten? the consideration of it strikes such a terror to my hart, that, my thinks, I have an apprehension at this instant, that while we are heer in deliberation, consulting of the lawes, by wch we might repress them, they are in act, laboring wth their instruments for the vndermining of those lawes by wch we doe consult. Such is growne their their bouldness such increases they have had by the remission of the lawes, what then a defection would induce, what would be the consequence of that a faction, we may easilie conclude. *adeo manifestum est* (as Tacitus saies in the like case) *neq perire, neq salvas esse nisi vna posse.* they are like Hippocrates twinns, borne vnder such a constellation, that the same passions doe affect them, & their inclinations are common & alike both vnto health, & sickness. soe as in the coniuncture 'tis apparant what great danger wee are in. Nor does the termination of our danger rest in this, in this double danger of rell: & our lib: (though in that it be too much & from wch I beseech the L. deliver vs) but it yet goes further & takes in a third concommitant, the danger of the K. the danger of the St. w^ch (as their is a mutuall involution of the others) is soe involv'd in them, that ther cannot be a preiudice to either, but this likewise must participat. ffor as a defection in our lawes prepares the way, & opens to a defection in rell: soe a defection in rell: would soone induce in the partisans therof a defection of their loyalties: the verie obiect of their faith & principle of their motions being obedience to the papacie, & the doctrines of the Jesuits, & both these leading (as their owne authorities confess it) to advance the Spa: greatness;

to erect that temporall Monarchie to the pretended latitude & extension of wch they assume for their spirituall, & to make it (answearable to the title they have given it)

Catholicke & Vniversall soe that to the danger of rell: & our lib: from the same reasons & necessities is added likewise the danger and dissaftie to the state.

from here then (   ) y^u may see the truth of that suggestion so often framd against vs, that our labors & agitations of these points, in the instances, & insistances we have made for rell : & the lib : we have studied onlie an opposition to the K & the scandall of the goverm^t : here y^u may see likewise the truth of that assertion, wch so farr prevailes against vs, that the lib : of the Kingdome are a diminution to regalitie : when the verie contraries are evident, that into the regall saftie the lib : of the Kingdome have a large power & influence : & that ther cannot be a more advantage to the K. or honor to the goverm^t. then the care & agitation of these points, naie further, this inferenc I will add, for a note & character of the opposits, that he that is not affectionat to these a frinde both to our rell : & our lib : what ever outward shewes or pretences may be vsd is secretlie & in hart noe frinde but enemie, (& when occasion is wilbe so ready to declare him) both to the K. & St.

this treble consideration of the State, of rell : of our lib : has' now calld me vp, the strickt' coniuncture is betweene them, & the necessities they are in : the importance of this pointe to have them rightlie apprihended, & the light it will diffuse, wch may have some reflection on his M^r : the prevention it may give to the detractions of our enemies, & the difficulties it may remove from the course of our proceedings (that noe false pretensions doe disturbe vs for order or precedenc, wherin, I fear, we have had noe small preiudice heertofore) these considerations, I say, have beene my occasion at this time, this indeavor flowing from the intention of my dutie, my dutie to y^r Service, my duty to my Countrie, my dutie [to] my Sover, my dutie vnto God; that generall obligation bindes vs all, in a cause of this necessitie has' exacted this expression, in w^{ch}, I hope, I cannot be mistaken.

& therfore I shall conclude wth this motion or desire, in respect of the great importance of the work; ther being such apparant dangers in rell: & our lib: & those soe trenching by reflection on the St. their coniuncture & dependance being such that the same dangers & necessities are common to them all, I shall desire (I say) that on those two principles we may pitch of rell. & our lib: that these may be the subiect of o^r treaties, & that heerin our cares may be equally divided, wthout anie preiudical affectation of either, & that by a firme & settled order of the house nothing may retard or interrupt vs but that in a constant & strickt' course we may keepe our intentions on these points, till they are well establisht'."

Subsidiary to this is a rough holograph draft of another Speech on the proposition of the Courtiers for a Fund. It thus runs:—

"The greatness & necessitie of this worke maks me thinke Fol. 34-35. it necessarie to vse some now towardℓ it: for not only the evills of guilt & punishment are before vs all things threatning wth miserie & affliction, all things crying for that iustice from above: but even the evills of o^r humiliation themselves, & our former solemnities I fear in those acts of humiliation, have beene evell wch requires some caution by the way, that we turne not our pieties to impiety. religion is the cheife virtue of a man, devotion of relligion, praier & fasting are the cheife characters of devotion, let these be corrupted in their vse, the devotion is corrupt: if the devotion be once taynted the religion is impure; it then becomes but an outward forme of godliness denying the power. & as its concluded in the text a religion that's in vaine, for such religion in this place, or at these times I impeach noe man let their owne consciences accuse them; of such devotion I make no iudgment vpon others, but leave them to the searcher of all harts ther only for caution I address that if we have beene guiltie in this kinde let vs now heer repent it. let vs remember that repentance is not in words, 'tis not by saying Lord, Lord we shall enter into heaven, but doing the will of our ffather wch is in heaven; & that doing is not by vndoing of our Countries, 'tis not that ffathers will that we should betray that mother; 'tis not a privat contract to the publicke breath & preiudice. but a sinceritie in all a through out integritie & perfection that our words & works be answearable, for y^t our actions correspond not to our words, noe iustice can perswade vs that successes shalbe better then our harts, wch when such neer kindred differ, strangers may be at odds. & the prevention of this evill is the cheife reason that I move for. nor is it wi^thout cause that this motion does proceed, if we reflect vpon the former passages of this place may might be thence collected to support the proprietie of this caution but the desire is better to reforme errors, then remember them. my affections strike for the happiness of this meeting, that must be had from god, 'tis his blessing though our crowne : Let vs fear him therefore in all sinceritie expect it, & if by vaine shadowes will delude vs, let vs distinguishe between true substances & those shews. 'tis religion not the name of religion that must guide vs, that in the truth. therof we may wth all vnitie be concordant not turning it into subtiltie & art playing wth god as wth the powers of men, but in the sincerity of our sowles doing that worke we come for wch I most humbly move & pray for that blessing from above."

[*See continuation of the Port Eliot MSS. in the Supplement to Vol. II. page* 111.]

END OF VOL. I.

CHISWICK PRESS:—C. WHITTINGHAM AND CO. TOOKS COURT, CHANCERY LANE.

www.ingramcontent.com/pod-product-compliance
Lightning Source LLC
Chambersburg PA
CBHW032226230426
43666CB00033B/1609